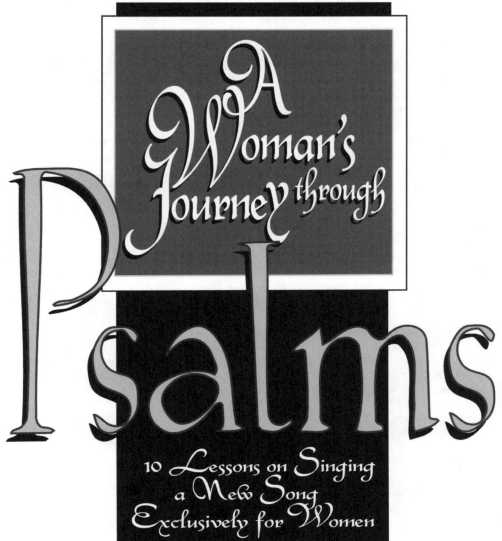

A Woman's Journey through Psalms

Psalms

10 Lessons on Singing a New Song Exclusively for Women

Titles by Dee Brestin

From Cook Communications

The Friendships of Women
The Friendships of Women Workbook
We Are Sisters
The Joy of Women's Friendships
The Joy of Eating Right
The Joy of Hospitality
A Woman of Joy
A Woman of Value
A Woman of Insight
A Woman's Journey through Luke
A Woman's Journey through Ruth
A Woman's Journey through Esther
A Woman's Journey through 1 Peter
My Daughter, My Daughter

From Harold Shaw/Waterbrook

Proverbs and Parables
Ecclesiastes
Examining the Claims of Christ (John 1-5)
1, 2 Peter and Jude
How Should a Christian Live? (1, 2, 3 John)
Higher Ground
Building Your House on the Lord
Friendship

From Word

Falling in Love with Jesus

Faithful Woman is an imprint of
Cook Communications Ministries, Colorado Springs, Colorado 80918
Cook Communications, Paris, Ontario
Kingsway Communications, Eastbourne, England

A WOMAN'S JOURNEY THROUGH PSALMS
©2001 by Women's Friendship Ministries

First Printing, 2001
Printed in the United States of America
CD produced in Singapore

1 2 3 4 5 6 7 8 9 10 Printing/Year 05 04 03 02 01

Editor: Dorian Coover-Cox
Design: Bill Gray
Cover Photo: Faust Reynolds

Contents

Acknowledgments   6

Introduction   7

Special Instructions for Preparation and Discussion   10

One: Shout to the Lord   13

Two: Planted by Streams of Water   26

Three: The Lord Is Close to the Brokenhearted   38

Four: Why Are You Downcast, O My Soul?   52

Five: Whiter Than Snow   64

Six: GIve Thanks   77

Seven: Under the Shadow of Your Wings   88

Eight: As a Father Has Compassion   100

Nine: I Hope in Your Word   112

Ten: I Was Made to Praise You   128

Sources   140

A Personal Note From the Author   143

A Woman's Journey through Psalms CD

1. "Shout to the Lord," Darlene Zschech
©1993 Darlene Zschech/Hillsong Publishing (Administered in the U.S. and Canada by Integrity's Hosanna! Music)/ASCAP
Singers: Integrity Worship Team
Spanish solo: Ingrid Rosario
From: Outrageous Joy/14232
2. "Streams of Water," Sy Gorieb and Tim Hosman
©1993 Integrity's Praise! Music/BMI and Integrity's Hosanna! Music/ASCAP
Soloists: Sy Gorieb, Frankie Montego and Rick Riso
From: Renewing Your Mind (Scripture Memory 16)/IMD316
3. "The Desire of the Afflicted," Danny Chambers
©1992 Integrity's Praise! Music/BMI
Soloist: Susie Stevens
From: Encouragement (Scripture Memory 07)/IMD307
4. "Why Are You Downcast," Danny Chambers
©1992 Integrity's Praise! Music/BMI
Soloist: Lenny LeBlanc
From: Encouragement (Scriputre Memory 07)/IMD307
5. "Whiter Than Snow," Bob Ayala
©1994 Integrity's Hosanna! Music/ASCAP
Soloist: Greg Barnhill
From: Shield of Faith (Scriputre Memory 25)/IMD325
6. "Give Thanks," Henry Smith
©1978 Integrity's Hosanna! Music/ASCAP
Soloist: Don Moen
From: My Life Is in You/ALD005
7. "Under the Shadow," Kent Henry and John Stevenson
©1988 Integrity's Hosanna! Music/ASCAP and Integrity's Praise! Music/BMI
Soloist: Kelly Willard
From: We Will Glorify/ALD003
8. "As a Father Has Compassion," Don Harris
©1993 Integrity's Hosanna! Music/ASCAP
Soloist: Cathy Riso
From: God's Love/IMD311
9. "I Hope in Your Word," Harlan Rogers
©1994 Integrity's Hosanna! Music/ASCAP
Soloist: Melodie Crittenden
From: Everlasting Hope/IMD326
10. "I Was Made to Praise You," Chris Christensen
©1988 Integrity's Hosanna! Music/ASCAP
Soloist: Karen Childers
From: I Was Made to Praise You/00832

Integrity Music. All recordings used courtesy of Integrity Incorporated. For information on products available from Integrity, please visit your Christian bookstore or contact Integrity by calling 1-800-533-6912 or visit www.integritymusic.com.

To Mother,

who sang the psalms to me

How I Thank God For:

The wonderful team at Integrity Music.
They have lived up to their name. Their foremost desire has been to provide a product that is honoring to You, Lord, and You have blessed them with amazingly gifted writers and musicians. A particular thanks for Don and Debra Mays, Margaret Middleton, and Wes Tuttle.

My editor at Dallas Theological Seminary, Dorian Coover-Cox.
Having a Hebrew scholar's point of view has been immeasurably helpful in keeping this guide true to the Word of God. As always, she has gone way above and beyond. Thank You, Lord, for Dorian's good mind and generous spirit.

My amazing assistant, Gay Tillotson.
How good of You, Lord, to provide me with such a talented and energetic assistant, gifted in administration *and* with people. And how merciful of You to provide me with an assistant who lies awake at night, praying, "How can we make this guide the best it can be?"

My prayer team.
Father, thank You for giving individuals the burden to pray for my writing, and in particular, for this guide. Without them, would we have had the same anointing of Your Spirit? Please bless them, Lord, for their intercessory prayers.

Greg Clouse of Cook Communications.
Lord, thank You for giving Greg the faith to believe in this project and the tenacity to hang on in the face of setbacks. You have rewarded His trust.

My husband.
How undeserving I am to have a man like Steve, who encourages, edifies, and daily prays that You would quicken me for this work. Thank You for leading him to Charles Spurgeon and giving him the desire to immerse himself in this godly man's writings on the Psalms. Thank You for Steve's contagious excitement and insightful input.

Charles Spurgeon.
So many years ago You quickened this man, this "Prince of Preachers," with a passion for the Psalms. You have richly blessed succeeding generations through him.

Introduction

"A longing fulfilled is sweet to the soul" (Proverbs 13:19a). That is what this study guide is for me. For years I prayed I could write a study on psalms accompanied by a recording with those same psalms set to music. I imagined women being uplifted and encouraged by these praise choruses as they were doing dishes, nursing their babies, or driving to work.

After all, the psalms were intended to be sung! David sang them with his harp, and throughout the ages they have been an inspiration for music. Our daughter Sally recently visited a church in the hills of Scotland where the congregation simply turned to the Book of Psalms and began to sing. The melodies had been passed down from generation to generation, and they sang lustily. Sally said, "They sounded like bagpipes, for they took deep breaths. The men sang with great fervor, and the women harmonized. So earnest were their hearts!" Some of our most outstanding contemporary praise choruses are simply psalms set to music. (It's hard to improve upon the divine songwriter.)

Jesus, as He often does, surpassed my dreams by allowing me to team with the amazingly gifted artists from *Integrity Music*. I am absolutely convinced that this study will profoundly deepen your love relationship with the Lord, not only for now, but for always, because the gift of music will forever etch these psalms on your heart. Long after the study is completed you will enjoy the Integrity compact disc, and it will help keep you "under the shadow of His wings."

In addition to the Scripture memory songs, you will hear a few favorite choruses reflecting themes from the Psalms. We open with a particularly anointed song I am hearing sung nearly every place I give a women's seminar: "Shout to the Lord." In *Falling in Love with Jesus*, a book I wrote with recording artist Kathy Troccoli, Kathy tells this story about "Shout to the Lord."

> One night a friend dragged me to a worship event in Nashville. I say dragged because I was in such a bad state of mind. I was tired of some of the battles in my soul. I was tired of injustices. I was just tired. I sat there with my arms folded, thinking, "Yeah, yeah, yeah, whatever." Then they started singing, "My Jesus, My Savior, Lord there is none like you . . . " and I could see myself starting to melt. I think it's those times more than ever that I grieve. He's so good and so kind and so gentle. His mercy pours over me as His love embraces me, and all my walls come tumbling down, and I see Him clearly.[1]

I am also hoping to introduce many of you to Charles Spurgeon, the "Prince of Preachers." Six years before he began his thirty-year preaching career (without a microphone!) in the six-thousand-seat Metropolitan Tabernacle of London, he was ministering in London in the time of cholera. This young pastor visited the sick constantly and conducted funerals daily. During the treacherous plague, Spurgeon clung to the psalms. He preached on them, prayed through them, and memorized them. He spent half of his adult life composing his commentary on the *Book of Psalms*, *The Treasury of David*. Upon completing this great work, he wrote,

> *A tinge of sadness is on my spirit . . . never to find on this earth a richer storehouse, though the whole palace of Revelation is open to me.*[2]

The Treasury of David is incomparable, in the opinion of many experts, to anything that has ever been written on the Psalms. My husband first introduced me to Spurgeon. After reading the three volume set, Steve said, "I have spent the last year in the company of a very godly man." I could see the deepening walk and love for God in my husband, and so I was drawn to the "Prince of Preachers" as well. Now I share Spurgeon with you—and not only Spurgeon, but the wealth of comments and quotes from the hundreds he drew upon, men and women with amazing hearts from centuries past.

In the *Woman's Journey* series, I have chosen books that are of particular interest to women: Esther, Ruth, Luke, 1 Peter, and now Psalms. Women love psalms for their beauty, their tenderness, and their poetry, and I will be looking at them from a woman's perspective, seeking applications that are particularly relevant to a woman's life.

The secret of a victorious Christian life is developing a heart like David's, the man who lived some three thousand years ago and in a variety of occupations: shepherd, court musician, warrior, fugitive, king of Israel, and author of most of the psalms. But David is known best as the man after God's heart. How do we develop a heart like this?

Study the psalms! You will discover David's highs and lows, his times of praise and his times of pain. But one thing is consistent, he is talking to the Love of his life. His dialogue with the Lord is continual. He so esteemed God that he ran to

Him constantly, longing for His guidance, His power, and His presence. Dallas Willard writes:

If you bury yourself in Psalms, you emerge knowing God and understanding life.[3]

By memorizing the choruses on the CD, you will be memorizing the prayers of the Psalms. As they become your prayers, you *will* develop a heart like David's. You will experience more power, more joy, and more confidence in God.

Special Instructions for Preparation and Discussion

Homework

As I travel across the country I am seeing a genuine hunger for in-depth Bible studies as women are discovering the power of the Word. No longer satisfied with "Christianity lite," they want to dig, to discover, and to deepen their walk with God.

A Women's Journey through Psalms is divided into five daily quiet times that should take about thirty minutes each to complete.

If you find yourself unusually rushed on a particular day, just read the text and the questions with the asterisks. These shortcuts will cause you to miss some wonderful views, but they are provided so that you do not give up on those frantic days (when the baby has a fever or you have a final exam). We want you to continue with us in the journey. However, don't take the shortcut because of laziness, or you will never develop the kind of heart for God that will give you inextinguishable joy.

If you are new to Bible study, the best way to establish a habit is to choose the same time and the same place each day and stick to it. As a young Christian I would not allow myself to read or watch anything before I'd had my time with the Lord. Soon it wasn't a discipline but a desire.

Discussion

These lessons can be discussed in ninety minutes. If you don't have that much time, you have two options:
1.   Do the whole lesson but discuss half the questions. (I prefer this as it increases your time in the Word. But some groups, such as young moms, may find this overwhelming.)
2.   Take twenty weeks to do this guide by dividing the lessons: Do the questions from the first three days one week and the questions from the last two days the second week. Do the prayer time each week.

The best discussions occur when everyone is prepared and has an opportunity to share what the Lord has taught her. If you are naturally talkative, discipline yourself to speak not more than four times. If you are naturally shy, mark places where you will speak up, at least twice. If you do not have your homework done, then allow the others to share and add only when they seem to be done.

Make yourself vulnerable as the Lord leads. Women who are unwilling to be honest sacrifice bonding and growth. During the prayer time, follow David's example and confess where you are struggling to live wholeheartedly for God. Get some prayer support to break those strongholds; don't just ask for prayer for Cousin Mary's gallbladder surgery. When other women make themselves vulnerable, show yourself worthy of their trust and keep confidences within the group.

The Psalms Compact Disc

Allow God to prepare your heart by listening to the praise chorus of the week daily, before you immerse yourself in the study. Then play the CD at other times, allowing these psalms to become etched upon your heart.

One

Shout to the Lord

$\mathcal{I}$ want a heart like David's, a joy like David's. Scholars throughout the ages have told us that a key to developing a heart like David's is to study the Psalms. No other book of the Bible gives us such an intimate look at the one who was called "a man after God's heart."

In his book *The Bible Jesus Read*, Philip Yancey confesses that, for many years, he avoided the Book of Psalms. True, there are some wonderfully comforting psalms, but there are also psalms of great pain, sorrow, and anger. When Yancey was looking for comfort, he would accidentally turn to one of the wintriest psalms and end up "frostily depressed."[1]

Yancey said that he had missed the main point, which was:

> *The book of Psalms comprises a sampling of spiritual journals, much like personal letters to God. . . . I must read them as an "over-the-shoulder" reader since the intended audience was not other people, but God.*[2]

David had a heart that yearned for God, for he absolutely knew that the secret to a joyful life was to have nothing between his Lord and himself. So when David was sad, he lamented to the Lord, when he was angry, he pleaded for justice, and when he was joyful, he sang and danced before the Lord. Though "Shout to the Lord" is a contemporary praise chorus, it isn't hard to imagine David singing something like it.

Shout to the Lord

My Jesus
My Savior
Lord, there is none like You
All of my days
I want to praise
The wonders of Your mighty love

My Comfort
My Shelter
Tower of refuge and strength
Let every breath
All that I am
Never cease to worship You

Shout to the Lord
All the earth let us sing
Power and majesty, praise to the King
Mountains bow down and the seas will roar
At the sound of Your name

I sing for joy
At the work of Your hand
Forever I'll love You, forever I'll stand
Nothing compares to the promise I have in You

Mi Cristo
Mi Rey
Nadie es como Tu
Toda mi vida
Quiero exaltar
Las maravillas de Tu amor

Consuelo
Refugio
Torre de fuerza y poder
Todo mi ser
Lo que yo soy
Nunca cese de adorar

The themes in "Shout to the Lord" are repeated in David's psalms. As you memorize this song, you will have the opportunity to set your heart to think, pray, and praise in ways that he did. This week you will do an introduction and an in-depth study of Psalms 22 and 18.

If you are doing this in a small group, you will start to get acquainted with the other women. Pray that this will be just the beginning of a sweet and rich fellowship. I have often found that God puts particular women together for a reason.

If possible, do this lesson ahead of time. If that is not possible, then do it together now. (If you are doing it together, you will need to take the shortcut. Answer only the questions with asterisks.)

*Warm-Up

Tell your name and a sentence about yourself. What are you looking forward to in this group?

Day 1: My Jesus, My Savior

The opening introductions are vital. Read them carefully.

*1.   Comment on what stood out to you from the
        *A. Introduction (pp. 7-9)

    *B. Special instructions for preparation and discussion (pp. 10-11)

Read the comment from Kathy Troccoli aloud from p. 7 in the introduction and then listen to "Shout to the Lord" from your first track on the compact disc. Listen to it again and sing along with it.

2.   "My Jesus, My Savior," from "Shout to the Lord" implies a sweet intimacy with the Almighty God. How do you see this kind of relationship in the following?
        *A. Psalm 5:1-3

B. Psalm 116:1-2

3.   What two thoughts together overwhelm David in Psalm 8:3-4?

*4.   Share, in one breath, a time when you were aware that the Lord was per-sonally "mindful" of you, when He "inclined His ear" to you. What will you share? (Hear from those who wish to share, giving others the freedom to pass.)

Day 2: Lord, There Is None Like You

Jesus told His disciples that everything that was written about Him in the prophets and the *psalms* had to be fulfilled (Luke 24:44). Many of the psalms are messianic psalms, pointing to Christ and to His uniqueness as the Savior, the Bridegroom, and the Reigning King. David focused on these qualities, and all of his days, David praised the Lord for who He was. Today we will study what Charles Spurgeon calls "the Psalm of the cross," a photograph of our Lord's saddest hours. "We should read reverently," Spurgeon says, "putting off our shoes from our feet, as Moses did at the burning bush, for if there be holy ground anywhere in Scripture it is in this Psalm."[3]

In Psalm 22, David described a time of terrible suffering that he experienced. He spoke of groaning and crying to God for help day and night. (vv. 1-2) The Lord Jesus and the writers of the New Testament knew this psalm well and saw that it also described Jesus' experiences. They recognized His suffering as the ultimate example of what David as a prophet described. Why did Jesus allow Himself to suffer so? Because of His great love for us.

Lord, there is none like You
All of my days
I want to praise
The wonders of Your mighty love

Listen to "Shout to the Lord." Sing along with it, beginning to memorize it.

*Read Psalm 22:1-21.
If you have two Bibles, you may want to leave one open to Psalm 22 while you turn to the fulfillment of its prophecies in the New Testament of the other.

5.   As an overview, describe how each of the following was fulfilled in Christ.
     *A. Psalm 22:1 (Matthew 27:46)

     B. Psalm 22:6-8 (Matthew 27:39-44)

     C. Psalm 22:15 (John 19:28)

The agony described in Psalm 22:14 and 15 was a result of the extreme cruelty of crucifixion. T. W. Hunt describes this in *The Mind of Christ.*

> *The weight of the body fixed certain breathing muscles in an inhalation state . . . the victim discovered that he could breathe in and not out. . . . If he used the nail going through his feet as a cruel step to force his body upward . . . he could breathe again. Each time Christ spoke, He had to do this. . . . His body became soaked in perspiration. From loss of blood and perspiration, dehydration became extreme and thirst became intense.*[4]

     *D. Psalm 22:16 (Matthew 27:27-31)

     *E. Psalm 22:17-18 (Luke 23:34-35)

*F. Psalm 22:22 (John 20:17)

*6.   Growing up, I thought being a Christian was being a "good person." Though I was familiar with the story of Jesus' death and resurrection, I didn't understand what it had to do with me. Read 1 Peter 2:24-25 and explain, as if you were explaining to a person like I was, what the death and resurrection of Jesus could mean to her.

*7.   If you have put your trust in the shed blood of Christ, *in one sentence*, tell what you did.

*8.   If you have put your trust in the shed blood of Christ, *in one sentence*, summarize how it has impacted you.

9.   There is a transition in Psalm 22:22 from the gloom of the crucifixion to the morning light of the resurrection morning. What reasons can you glean for the joy?

The transition at v. 22 is now understood not in deliverance from death, as was the case for the psalmist, but in deliverance through death, achieved in the resurrection. And it is that deliverance which is the ground of praise, both for the sufferer (vv. 23-27) and for the "great congregation" (vv. 28-32).[5]
Peter Craigie

Day 3: My Comfort, My Shelter

Rebecca Pippert tells a story of her life being threatened when she was a college girl. On her flight home for Christmas, she had a five-hour layover in St. Louis and decided to take a cab to a mall for a few hours. As quickly as she stepped into the unmarked car (the driver claimed his cab was in the shop), she realized this man was not a cabby at all. As they drove out, away from the city, into a deserted area, Rebecca prayed desperately to God for help. The thought that came to her was, "Tell him of My love."

> I began to talk a mile a minute. I told him about me, how I had become a Christian, and even what the Lord had done in my life. I shared that I was going home for Christmas and couldn't wait to see my parents and brother and sister. I asked him to tell me about himself and his family, though he did not answer. Never mind! I talked enough for both of us. Then there was a chilling moment. He pulled the car to the side of the road and stared at me through the rearview mirror. There was nothing more I could say, and so I waited in silent prayer. After what felt like an eternity, he turned the car around and without ever saying a word, drove me to the shopping mall and dropped me off. . . .

> I could not stop shaking once I knew I was safe. I called a real taxi service and returned to the airport immediately. I told the driver what had happened and of course he lectured me severely about being so foolish as to get into an unmarked car. Then he said, "Now I need to tell you something. Last week at this airport a pleasant looking man told a young woman that his taxi was in the shop, and that he needed the money badly. And she fell for it. Then he took her to a country road and raped and stabbed her repeatedly. She's in critical condition at the hospital and the police haven't been able to find him. Let me tell you, girly, Somebody up there likes you."[6]

The psalm we will study for the rest of this week, Psalm 18, is a glorious psalm of God's great deliverance. When His child cries desperately for help, it is as if she has rung the alarm bell in heaven. The poet David portrays Almighty God thundering in the heavens and then descending to earth in the storm clouds, firing bolts of lightning, and sending enemies running in dread fear. This is a psalm showing God's deliverance of His child, who could be David, you, or me.

When King Saul realized David's popularity and God's anointing upon him, Saul was extremely jealous and tried to murder him. David spent almost twenty years as a fugitive—running, hiding in forests, damp caves, and mountain crags. Yet again and again, as David cried out to God and trusted Him, God came running to help His child, delivering him from the hand of his enemies. Psalm 18 was written by David, perhaps near the end of his life. Its placement in 2 Samuel 22 suggests that it is a fitting review of David's remarkable history and a grateful retrospect on how the Lord had been his Comfort, his Shelter.

Listen to "Shout to the Lord" again. Can you sing it by heart?

10.   What do you imagine it would feel like to be a fugitive, to be constantly on the run, hiding from your enemies? (There also may be someone, such as a missionary, in your group who has actually experienced this.)

11.   Our real enemies are spiritual, for we do not wrestle against flesh and blood, but against . . . the rulers of darkness of this world (Ephesians 6:12). Our enemy prowls around, telling us lies, sowing discord, tempting us in the areas where we are weak (1 Peter 5:8). Describe a spiritual battle you have fought and won, or one you are waging now.

12.   In Psalm 18, David is remembering the many times he ran to the Lord and found Him to be his tower of refuge. Reviewing God's faithfulness in the past helps us to trust Him in the present. How do you see this in David's argument in 1 Samuel 17:37, as to why he, though he was just a boy, could fight Goliath?

The following verses appear in a familiar praise chorus. If you know it, sing it now to the Lord in your quiet time. (The psalms were meant to be sung!)

> I will call upon the LORD,
> who is worthy to be praised:
> so shall I be saved from my enemies . . .
> The LORD liveth; and blessed be my rock;
> and let the God of my salvation be exalted.
> Psalm 18:3, 46 (KJV)

*13. How does David open Psalm 18? (vv. 1-2) In what recent circumstances has the Lord been a comfort, a shelter, or a deliverer to you?

*14. Notice the repetition of the word "my" in verse 2. List each of the "my's."

15. In describing his distress, David vividly paints his desperation. Look carefully at the metaphors, the word pictures. What do you see in Psalm 18:4-5?

It has been supposed by some, that the allusion is to the ancient mode of hunting wild animals. A considerable tract of country was surrounded with strong ropes. The circle was gradually contracted, till the object of pursuit was so confined as to become an easy prey for the hunter. These cords were the cords of death, securing the death of the animal.[7]
John Brown

16. What kind of emotion and fervency accompanied the prayer in Psalm 18:6?

Our prayers are cordial, modest, even reverent. Eugene Peterson calls them "cut-flower prayers." They are not like Jesus' prayers, or, for that matter, like the psalms. The ranting and raving, the passion and ecstasy, the fury and desolation found in the psalms are so far from our religious expression that it seems hard to believe they were given to us as our guide to prayer.[8]
John Eldredge

Day 4: Mountains Bow Down and the Seas Will Roar
After living outdoors, keeping his sheep, watching furious thunderstorms from

the shelter of a cave, the poet David now draws upon these images to describe his Father's strong response to His child's cry. How I love the poetry from Psalm 18 that we are studying today. The beautiful images in verses 4-19 are like the images in "Shout to the Lord."

> *Mountains bow down and the seas will roar*
> *At the sound of Your name.*

17.   Meditate on Psalm 18:7-19.
   *A. What description of the Lord's powerful response is in verse 7?

Observe how the most solid and immovable things feel the force of supplication. Prayer has shaken houses, opened prison doors, and made stout hearts to quail. Prayer rings the alarm bell, and the Master of the house arises to the rescue, shaking all things beneath his tread. . . . Nothing makes God so angry as an injury done to his children.[9]
Charles Spurgeon

*B. Describe the images of God coming to the rescue in
   v. 8

   v. 9

   v. 10

   vv. 11-14

Every thunderstorm should remind us of God's exhibition of power and vengeance.[10]
George Horne (1730-1791)

C. What picture of the earth is given in verse 15 because of God's anger?

In order to thoroughly appreciate the beauty [of this passage] . . . we should endeavor to realise the full power of an Oriental storm. Solitary lightning

precedes the discharge—this is meant by the coals in verse 8: the clouds approach the mountain summits—"the heavens bow," as verse 9 has it; the storm shakes its pinions; enwrapped in thick clouds as in a tent . . . He speaks, and thunder is his voice; he shoots, and flashes of lightning are his arrows. At his rebuke, and at the blast of his breath the earth recedes—the sea foams up, and its beds are seen—the land bursts, and the foundations of the world are discovered. And lo! An arm of deliverance issues forth from the black clouds, and the destructive fire grasps the wretched one who had cried out from the depths, pulls him forth, and delivers him from all his enemies.[11]
Augustus F. Tholuck (1856)

Day 5: Forever I'll Stand

Eric Liddel was an Olympic runner who loved God and refused to run on Sundays. His faithfulness to the Lord won the admiration of many. A fellow runner, a Jew, sent him a note of encouragement. It said:

To the faithful you show yourself faithful,
to the blameless you show yourself blameless,
Psalm 18:25

The Lord is just in His dealings with men and women. With the merciful, He is merciful, with the faithful, He is faithful, with the crooked, He is shrewd. No standard could be fairer than the one we find expressed in Psalm 18:25-26.

Christ was without sin, so it is easy to see Him in verses 20-24, but what about David and us? David sinned greatly, yet he was "blameless" in the scriptural sense. (When he was made aware of sin he repented wholeheartedly, and got back into the light.)

Meditate on Psalm 18:20-28.
*18. Describe God's rule of fairness.

Read Psalm 18:29-50.
19. What does God do that no one else can do?

*20. Contrast God's response to David's cry for help (vv. 16-19; vv. 32-40) with His response to David's enemies' cry for help (vv. 40-41).

The implication may either be that the enemies were Israelites and so called upon the Lord for help, or else that they were foreign enemies who called upon the Lord for help when no help was forthcoming from their own gods. . . . But the enemies' plans were to no avail; unlike the psalmist, they were not in such a relationship to God that they could expect the Lord's help when they cried, as could the psalmist (vv. 21-31).[12]
Peter Craigie

21. How close are you to the Lord, according to Psalm 18:21-31?

*22. For what does David praise the Lord in verses 33-36?

To the faithful, God shows Himself faithful, bringing that child to greater heights, increasing her strength, her victory, and her joy. Often we are afraid to die to ourselves, whatever that may mean in our lives. We are afraid there will not be a resurrection. We are afraid that if we obey, whether it is refraining from sexual immorality, overeating, or poor video choices, that life won't be fun. We may be hesitant to spend ourselves on behalf of the hungry or to minister to our elderly grandparents, thinking that we won't be happy. But we are deceived, for with every death there *is* a resurrection. Every step we take in obedience to the Lord takes us higher, and He makes our feet as surefooted as a mountain goat.

What a God he is! How perfect in every way!
All his promises prove true.
He is a shield for everyone who hides behind him.
For who is God except our Lord? Who but he is as a rock?
He fills me with strength and protects me wherever I go.
He gives me the surefootedness of a mountain goat upon the crags.
He leads me safely along the top of the cliffs.
Psalm 18:30-33 (TLB)

*23. What do you think you will remember about this week's lesson?

In your quiet time, sing "Shout to the Lord."

Prayer Time

The psalms were meant to be prayed. One of the most effective ways to pray is to speak the psalm aloud, allowing it to be the springboard for sentence prayers. The following is a sample of how it might happen in a small group:

Jean reads: *I love you, O Lord, my strength* (Psalm 18:1).

Beth prays: *I love you, O Lord.*

Shirley prays: *You are my strength. How I need your strength as I face my bad temper with my children.*

Jean prays: *O Lord, give Shirley strength.*

Silence

Beth reads the next verse, and the pattern is repeated.

Now it is your turn. Use the following verses as springboards for prayer.

I love you, O Lord, my strength.

Pray sentence prayers. When there is a silence, someone should read:

The Lord is my rock, my fortress and my deliverer;
my God is my rock, in whom I take refuge.

Pray sentence prayers.
Close by singing "Shout to the Lord" together.

Two

Planted by Streams of Water

hen we lived in the Pacific Northwest, my husband and I loved to take our little boys to the Oregon coast for a weekend. The closer we drove to the water, the more enveloped we became in green, green mansions. Lovely evergreens grew so tall they seemed to touch the boundaries of heaven. Every spring, tender green buds appeared, new fruit, new growth, always, in its season.

Now we live in Nebraska, surrounded by prairie. Everywhere are fields of corn, milo, and wheat. The chaff is the dry part of the stalk that is blown away. Dry, worthless, and gone with the wind.

That contrast is the picture given in the first psalm, which has been called the Book of Psalms in a nutshell. The godly man or woman is like a tree planted by the water, but the ungodly man or woman is like the chaff the wind blows away.

Warm-Up
Think about a tree that is particularly beautiful to you. What about it is appealing? What is one way you would like to be like that tree?

Day 1: Planted by Streams of Water
Psalm 1 is one of the most beloved and memorized passages in the Scripture. J. Vernon McGee divides the psalm into three parts:

1. The *practice* of the godly person
2. The *power* of the godly person
3. The *permanency* of the godly person[1]

The practice, power, and permanency of a godly person are brought to life through a vivid word picture: a tree planted by streams of water. Memorizing the opening three verses of Psalm 1 will be beautifully facilitated through the song "Streams of Water." The calypso drums of the song creatively transport us to the balmy breezes of a tropical island. Picture yourself in a hammock strung between two lush palm trees planted beside the blue, blue waters of the Caribbean. Listen to the song several times (track 2) and follow along with the lyrics, which follow Psalm 1:1-3 exactly.

Streams of Water

Blessed is the man
Who does not walk
In the counsel of the wicked
Or stand in the way of sinners
Or sit in the seat of mockers
But his delight
Is in the law of the Lord
And on His law
He meditates day and night

He is like a tree
Planted by streams of water
(Repeat 3 times)

Which yeilds its fruit in season
And whose leaf does not wither
Whose leaf does not wither
Whatever he does prospers

Sy Gorieb and Tim Hosman
© 1993 Integrity's Praise! Music/BMI and Integrity's Hosanna! Music/ASCAP
Soloists: Sy Gorieb, Frankie Montego, and Rick Riso

Read Psalm 1.
*1.   List the characteristics of the tree.

2.   This tree is planted by the streams of water. Turn to Isaiah 55.
      A. What invitation is made, and for what reason in verses 1-2?

B. What impact does water have on the earth in verse 10?

C. To what is God's Word compared in verses 10-11? How are they alike?

D. What promise is given in verse 11?

E. What contrast is given in Isaiah 55:13? How is this like Psalm 1?

*3.   What is the *practice* or the habit of the godly person according to Psalm 1:2? List everything you can discover from this verse.

4.   As you are establishing the way of life described in Psalm 1:1-2, can you see a specific way the Lord has brought forth fruit? (The glory goes to the Lord, and the group will be encouraged if you share an area where you have seen victory.)

*5.   Contemplate your *practice* or habit of drawing from the water of God's Word.
   *A. When do you plan to do your lesson each day?

   *B. Where will you do your lesson?

*C. How might you use the CD in times other than just when working on your lesson?

*D. How does it help you when the other women in the group have done their lessons carefully? How does it hurt you when they haven't?

Day 2: Does Not Walk, Stand, or Sit

The Book of Psalms begins with the way to blessedness. There are paths to be avoided, and paths to be taken. Psalm 1:1 begins with the paths to be avoided.

Dallas Willard compares the person who walks in the counsel of the wicked to the airplane pilot who gets disoriented and thinks he is flying up, higher into the sky, when he is really flying upside down and will plunge into the earth to his death. He has absolutely no idea that he is so turned around until he meets destruction.[2]

*6.   Give some examples of the counsel of the ungodly.

"The counsel of the wicked" is opposed to the Word of God. Wendy Shalit, a young Jewish girl at Williams College, caused a stir when she wrote A Return to Modesty. The counsel of immodesty, of promiscuous sex, was everywhere among her peers, even her professors, and in most women's magazines. She observed the misery of her female peers who were "unhappy with their bodies, with their sexual encounters, with the way men treat them on the street—unhappy with their lives." She concluded that many of "the woes besetting young women . . . are expressions of a society which has lost its respect for female modesty."[3]

*7.   How might walking in the counsel of the ungodly bring pain? Can you share an example from your own life?

Listen to the praise chorus and memorize the first half of verse 1.

Blessed is the man
Who does not walk
In the counsel of the wicked
Or stand in the way of sinners
Or sit in the seat of mockers

Read Psalm 1:1 in *Today's English Version, the Good News Bible.*

Happy are those
Who reject the advice of evil men,
Who do not follow the example of sinners
Or join those who have no use for God

8.   There is a downward progression in this verse. List the three steps down and explain why they are progressive.

Jill Savage, the founder of Hearts at Home, rejected the counsel of the world that said a young woman who stayed at home with her children was wasting her talents, and that someone else could mother her children just as well as she. Scripture stresses that children are a blessing of the Lord (Psalm 127:3) and that the godly parent disciples these precious treasures in the way of godliness (Deuteronomy 6:4-9). Jill did not stand in the path the world advised, nor did she join those who scoffed at stay-at-home moms. Instead, she immersed herself in studying Scripture, praying for her children, and in seizing teachable moments with them. She made their house a home. She filled it with love and laughter. Her children are becoming young people of strength and remarkable godliness. As they grew, Jill met with other women to pray about how to encourage other young mothers. The result? The tremendous ministry of Hearts at Home. Jill's model has become an inspiration to thousands of young mothers. She is like the fruitful and lovely tree of Psalm 1.

9.   To what is the godly wife compared in Psalm 128:3? And her children?

Hundreds of times have I seen the young olive plants spring up around the parent stem, and it has always made think of this verse. . . . The figure is very striking, and would be sure to present itself to the mind of every observer in the olive country. How beautiful to see the gnarled olive, still bearing abundant fruit, surrounded with a little band of sturdy successors, any one of which would be able to take its place should the central olive be blown down, or removed in any other way.[4]

Charles Spurgeon

Day 3: But Her Delight

In my own life, the more time I have spent with the Lord and in His Word, the more I have longed for Him. It has been so sweet, so satisfying, that I hunger for more. As a young believer, my spiritual life took a giant leap forward the summer I decided to study intensely the Book of Proverbs. I spent an hour or two in study each day. To my amazement, my relationship with my husband, my small sons, and my friends began to improve dramatically. My own joy and peace multiplied. The promises to the one who studies Proverbs (found in 1:1-6) and the promise of Psalm 1 began to be fulfilled in my life. The result? I wanted more. I had tasted and seen that the Lord was good, and I desired more.

As you study the Book of Psalms you will discover individuals who thirsted after God. This sort of person *delights* in the law of the Lord, and she meditates on it day and night. This truth of Psalm 1 is expanded on in Psalm 63. We will study this psalm today, but first, to prepare your heart, sing the first verse and the chorus of "Streams of Water." (Practice until you can do it without looking at the lyrics.)

10.   How do you see the thirst for the Word of God in Psalm 1:2?

Delighting in the Lord and His Word and meditating on it means, as Dr. Moffat explains, "to pour over" the Word.[5] It is far more than simply reading. It means looking carefully for comparisons, contrasts, promises, key words, repetitions, and warnings. It means considering cross references. It means memorizing it, and, especially in the case of Psalms, singing it. It means availing yourself of the best commentaries.

*11.   What have you done to help yourself "pour over" God's Word?

Another factor causing us to thirst for God is being in the wilderness. It is in the hard times that we thirst for the only One with the wisdom and the power to help us. Psalm 63 was probably written by David when he was fleeing the troops of his son Absalom. Absalom was intent on killing his father and taking his place as king. Hiding in a dry and weary land, David cried out to God.

Read Psalm 63.

12.   How does David describe his longing for God in verse 1? What word picture does David give?

13.   What has caused you to thirst for God and His Word?

If you know the praise chorus "Thy Lovingkindness" sing it now in your quiet time. It was inspired by Psalm 63:3-4.

14.   To what does David compare the goodness of the Lord in Psalm 63:5? What can you learn from this?

15.   When the psalmist is awake at night, what does he do, according to Psalm 63:6-7?

> *Lying awake, the good man betook himself to meditation, and then began to sing. He has a feast in the night, and a song in the night. . . . Night is congenial, in its silence and darkness, to a soul which would forget the world, and rise to a higher sphere.*[6]
> Charles Spurgeon

16.   What do you do when you lie awake in the night?

Day 4: Her Leaf Will Not Wither

Wouldn't you love to be the kind of woman whose life is absolutely guaranteed to make a difference, to count for eternity? And wouldn't you love to know, that no matter how old you get, or how wrinkled, or whenever you decide to go gray, that you will be lovely? People, and more importantly God, will say, "How beautiful she is, how pleasing her life!" The promise of Psalm 1 is that the practice of the godly woman will lead to power—fruit in its season, leaves that do not wither, and prosperity in all she does.

Listen to "Streams of Water" and learn the second verse.

*17.   List the three promises of power for the godly woman given in Psalm 1:3b.

18.   In every life there will be seasons of suffering, of trial, and of sweetness. In each of these seasons, the godly woman will bear fruit. Trace the fruit you would expect to see in a godly woman during a season of suffering, according to Romans 5:3-4.

In *The Hiding Place*, Corrie ten Boom tells of the fruit she saw in the season of suffering in her sister Betsie's life. Corrie accompanied Betsie, who was cough-ing up blood, on her frequent visits to the concentration camp hospital.

> *I hated the dismal place full of sick and suffering women, but we had to go back, again and again, for Betsie's condition was growing worse. She was not repelled by the room as I was. To her it was simply a setting in which to talk about Jesus—as indeed was every place else. Wherever she was, at work, in the food line, in the dormitory, Betsie spoke to those around her about His nearness and His yearning to come into their lives. As her body grew weaker, her faith seemed to grow bolder. And sick call was "such an important place, Corrie! Some of these people are at the very threshold of heaven!"*[7]

19. If you are in a season of suffering now, how could you apply the principles of Romans 5:3-4?

20. The verb for "prospers" in Psalm 1:3 is the same that describes Joseph. What do you learn about godly prosperity in Genesis 39:2-3 and 23?

21. What contrast do you find in the trees in the following passages?
     A. Isaiah 1:30

     B. Hosea 14:4-8

The fruitful tree of Psalm 1, whose leaves do not wither, is an evergreen, like a pine tree, a palm tree, or an olive tree—always green, lush, and fruitful in its season, as long as it has plenty of water, as this one did. Likewise, godly women, who are continually watered by the Word, maintain a radiance that cannot be robbed by age.

22. How are godly women described in the following passages?
     A. Proverbs 31:28-31

     B. 1 Peter 3:3-5

Day 5: They Are like the Chaff

Sometimes it doesn't seem that those in the world have chosen the wrong path. They seem to be flourishing, they seem to be loved. Open any secular women's magazine and you will see pictures of gorgeous women and read articles about their breathtaking romances, luxurious homes, or beauty secrets. Even within the church, often it may be the wealthy or the beautiful who are given the positions of honor, rather than those truly devoted to God.

We see, as the *King James Version* so picturesquely puts it, as if "through a glass, darkly" (1 Corinthians 13:12a). We may, in fact, completely misinterpret what we think we see. But one day the light will shine, one day we will see as God does, and one day we will see the missing piece: eternity. Those who were thought to be successful in the world will be gone, like the worthless, lifeless chaff the wind blows away. Those truly devoted to God will be standing, splendid and tall, for God has watched over them. We will wish we had invested more in eternity and less in the transitory, and we will wonder why we ever, ever envied those who were not truly devoted to God.

Read Psalm 1:4-6 in your translation and again in *The Living Bible*.

> *But for sinners, what a different story! They blow away like chaff before the wind. They are not safe on Judgment Day; they shall not stand among the godly. For the Lord watches over all the plans and paths of godly men, but the paths of the godless lead to doom.*

*23. List the dooms of the wicked.

Charles Spurgeon preached a sermon called "The Chaff Driven Away" on October 23, 1859, and many, many souls came to Christ. Here are excerpts from this famous sermon, preached by the "Prince of Preachers."

> *And who are the ungodly? . . . a man may be religious, yet not be godly . . . to be godly is to have a constant eye to God, to recognize him in all things, to trust him, to love him, to serve him. . . .*
>
> *The righteous man is like a tree planted by the rivers of water . . . but not so you that are ungodly, not so. Your days of drought shall come. You may rejoice now, but what will you do upon the bed of sickness, when fever shall make you toss from side-to-side, when head and heart shall be racked with anguish, when death shall stare upon you, and shall glaze your eyes? What will ye do when ye come into the swellings of Jordan? You have joys today, but where will be your joys then?*[8]

24.   What wonderful promise is given at the close of Psalm 1 to the godly? What does this mean to you right now?

25.   Psalm 37 expands upon Psalm 1. Read Psalm 37 in its entirety, visualizing its word pictures in your imagination.
    A.   What is the practice of the godly person according to verses 3 and 4? The result?

    B.   Often the psalms have what is called "an ascent." One precept leads to a higher one. How can you see this in Psalm 37:3-4?

Most believers have Jesus as their Savior, and perhaps as their King—but not as the Love of their life. They often trust Him, but seldom do they really delight in Him. They do not wake in the morning, rush into His arms, and wait for His kisses. (A kiss from the king, according to Rabbinic tradition, is a living word of prophecy. When Scripture leaps out at you and ministers to your need for that moment, you have been kissed by the King.) Most believers do not memorize His Word, meditate on it, sing songs in the night to Him, or practice His presence throughout the day. But, oh, the joys for those who delight in the Lord!

    C.   How do you understand the promise of Psalm 37:4b?

    D.   Why shouldn't we fret about the prosperity of the wicked? Find several word pictures that vividly show their lack of permanency.

E.   What promises to the godly from Psalm 37 are meaningful to you?

*26. What do you think you will remember about this week's lesson?

In your quiet time, sing "Streams of Water."

Prayer Time

When praying through Scripture together, be brave and personal, lifting up your own need so that your sisters can support you. Your vulnerability will encourage them to be honest and open as well. Small circles of three or four facilitate vulnerability. The following is an example:

> *But his delight is in the law of the Lord,*
> *And on his law he meditates day and night.*

> Amy: *Father, I confess I have not been delighting in your Word. Please give me a hunger for it.*

> Ellen: *Yes, Lord. Please give Amy great joy during her time with You.*

> Barbara: *I agree, Lord.*

> Silence

> Ellen then lifts up her need.

Following the above pattern, pray through Psalm 1:1. When there is a silence, pray through Psalm 1:2. Close by praying through Psalm 1:3.

Three

The Lord Is Close
to the Brokenhearted

My Bible says that I am the Lord's beloved, His bride. But sometimes it doesn't feel like that. Often I feel like the princess in a fairy tale where a storm comes to the forest, a tree crashes across my path, and a fire-breathing dragon appears.

I look around in a panic. Where is my Prince?

Just this month, a storm came to my forest. A phone call came telling me my father had found my eighty-eight-year-old mother on the floor next to the bed, unconscious. Unable to revive her, he called 911. Then she was in a San Diego hospital on life support.

Mothers are special. Mothers are irreplaceable.

My first plane was late, and I had ten minutes to make my next one. I ran through the Denver airport, weeping openly, wanting so to see her again on this earth. All the while I was praying: *Jesus, O sweet Jesus, please help us.*

I did make my plane. And my beautiful mother was still alive. When I entered her room and spoke to her, she began to toss and turn, nearly pulling the tubes from her mouth. Immediately I began quoting the song, actually Psalm 27:1, that I had heard her sing when I was a child:

The Lord is my light, and my salvation
Whom then shall I fear?
Whom then shall I fear?

The Lord is the strength of my life
The Lord is the strength of my life
Of whom then shall I be afraid?

She quieted. Then she pressed my hand. Our Prince was there.

The next day Mother woke up. She spoke words of love to me, to my father, and to my sisters. She smiled her sweet warm smile.

This time, Jesus stilled the storm. Sometimes, I know, He stills His child instead. But He always, always comes. He is near to the brokenhearted. He hears the cry of His children. And no matter our troubles, He delivers us from them all.

How can I say He delivers us from them all? People who genuinely love the Lord suffer. They battle with cancer, death, and an unfair world. And sometimes, they lose the battle.

The question is not our circumstances, but, is God in our circumstances? Is He near? Does He hear our cry? Does He find a way to encourage us? Does He eventually, *in His time*, deliver us from them all?

Yes. Oh, yes. Our Prince always comes through. And He is no fairy tale.

You will be strengthened to face your inevitable storms by memorizing "The Desire of the Afflicted," a song that contains thoughts from Psalms 10 and 34. Psalm 34 is a favorite of many, and we will study it in depth. How it will bless you!

Warm-Up
Think about a time when Jesus quieted the storm or quieted you. In one breath, share what happened.

Day 1: You Hear, O Lord, the Desire of the Afflicted
Abandoned as a baby, missing her left arm, Beth grew up in an orphanage in Bangkok, Thailand. As her tenth birthday approached, she began to give up hope that she would ever be adopted, for she knew that homes were seldom found for children over ten. She began to withdraw, going into a depression, frequently weeping.

It was at this time that my husband had a strong leading to consider adopting a child with special needs. When we prayed together, he had the strange sensation of hearing a girl weeping.

Through amazing circumstances Beth was brought to our attention. We are absolutely convinced that God, who places the solitary in families, placed Beth in our home. Psalm 10:17-18 tells us,

> *You hear, O LORD, the desire of the afflicted;*
> *you encourage them, and you listen to their cry,*
> *defending the fatherless and the oppressed,*
> *in order that man, who is of the earth, may terrify no more.*

Listen to track 3 on your disc.

The Desire of the Afflicted

You hear, O Lord, the desire of the afflicted
You encourage them and You listen to their cry
The Lord is close to the brokenhearted
And saves those who are crushed in spirit
A righteous man may have many troubles
But the Lord delivers him from them all
The Lord delivers him from them all
The Lord delivers him from them all
The Lord delivers him from them all

Danny Chambers
© 1992 Integrity's Praise! Music/BMI
Soloist: Susie Stevens

*1.   What stood out to you from the introduction?

Psalms 9 and 10 are often taken as a unit. One theme they share is the affliction of the righteous by the wicked. The righteous man may have many troubles, and often, it is at the hands of those whom Peter Craigie calls "practical atheists," people who may not claim to be atheists, but who behave as if there were no God.[1] We suffer in this world, and often those who are vulnerable, such as the orphan and the widow, are taken advantage of by the "strong." The word translated "afflicted" or "humble" in 10:17 has the idea of being "low in mind or circumstances." Therefore, the concept includes not just people who are socially oppressed, but also people who *humbly* realize their neediness and cry out to God.

Read Psalms 9 and 10 as an overview.

*2.   Psalm 9 closes with a contrast between the "wicked" and the "needy" around the concept of "forgetting." Find it in verses 17-18.

*3.   What promises can you find for the afflicted or the "humble" in the following verses?
    A. Psalm 9:12

    B. Psalm 9:18

Needy souls fear that they are forgotten . . . Satan tells poor tremblers that their hope shall perish, but they have here divine assurance . . . they do not wait in vain.[2]
                        Charles Spurgeon

    C. Psalm 10:14

    D. Psalm 10:17

Commenting on Psalm 10:17, Thomas Watson said, "God heareth not words, but desires."[3] What a comfort this is to me, for I often have not prayed well. I wish I had been wiser, more discerning, and used Scripture more when I prayed for my children as a young mother. And yet God heard my desires. He looks upon the young mother, the afflicted, and the humble woman who is crying out to Him and considers not so much her words, but her heart's desire.

Personal Prayer Time
Get on your knees and confess any sin humbly before God, and repent, truly. Tell Him your desires, your needs.

*Memorize Psalm 10:17 (NIV), using the song to help you.

Day 2: Those Who Look to Him Are Radiant
Psalm 34 was one of the first passages I memorized as a new believer. My husband was doing a medical internship in Seattle and was gone most nights. I was frightened to be alone with our babies at night in the city. I memorized Psalm 34, claimed its promises, and it ministered to me so. The Lord delivered me from my fears and I slept peacefully. Because Psalm 34 is in my heart, it has continued to minister to me over the last thirty years. This psalm is arranged alphabetically in Hebrew. The acrostic helped as a memory device; so this psalm was meant to be memorized. How you will be blessed if you memorize it all.

The first ten verses are a lovely hymn beginning with David's commitment to praise the Lord at all times. No matter how you are feeling, no matter the circumstances you may be facing, follow David's example and begin your personal quiet time with praise. Today, begin with "Shout to the Lord," and let your heart join in with your lips.

Read Psalm 34 in its entirety, as an overview.
4.   What particularly stands out to you upon this first reading?

*5.   What phrases in Psalm 34:1-2 show David's intent and determination?

6.   What similar thoughts do you find in the following passages?
      A. Psalm 92:1-4

Note that a line from "Shout to the Lord" follows Psalm 92:4.

      B. Ephesians 5:19-20

Psalm 34 was written by David after he was delivered from Achish (his official title was Abimelech). David, who spent much of his life as a fugitive from Saul, had been hiding in caves in the wilderness and had gotten weak and discouraged, not only in body, but in faith. Instead of looking to God for deliverance, he traveled west to the land of the Philistines, looking for help from the pagan ruler Achish.

7.   Read 1 Samuel 21:10–22:1.
      A. How did David's plight become worse when he went to Achish?

      B. What did David do?

When David escaped and returned to the wilderness of Israel to hide, I think he was lying there in the safety of the cave, thinking, I should have trusted God.[4]
J. Vernon McGee

So often I have made a difficult situation worse because I have trusted in my own devices instead of in God. Yet God in His mercy has not deserted me, and has listened to my cry. Recently I had a friend tell me, "Dee, when we get ourselves into a bad situation because of foolishness, I don't think that we should then ask God to get us out."

I responded, "You've just wiped out half my prayer life." Spurgeon writes, *We may seek God even when we have sinned. If sin could blockade the mercy-seat it would be all over for us.*[5]

*8.   For what specifically does David praise the Lord in Psalm 34:4?

If you restrain prayer, it is no wonder the mercy promised is retained. . . . fly thee to the throne of grace, and spread it before the Lord.[6]
                              William Gurnall (1617-1679)

*9.   What wonderful twofold promise is given in Psalm 34:5?

10.   David never boasted of his own devices. What should we boast in, according to Psalm 34:2? Compare this to Jeremiah 9:23-24.

11.   Who, according to Psalm 34:2b, will hear our praises and rejoice? Why is this important? How can this take place?

Sing "The Desire of the Afflicted" (track 3) in your quiet time. Can you sing the first four lines (Psalm 10:17) without looking at the words?

You hear, O Lord, the desire of the afflicted
You encourage them and You listen to their cry
The Lord is close to the brokenhearted
And saves those who are crushed in spirit

Day 3: The Angel of the Lord Encamps Around Those Who Fear Him

The wonderful promise that "the angel of the Lord encamps around those who fear him" is in Psalm 34:7, and it is a promise we have claimed for ourselves, for our children, and now, for our grandchildren. John Calvin wrote,

> *God has innumerable legions of angels who are always ready for His service . . . and are ever intent upon the preservation of our life, because they know that this duty is entrusted to them.*[7]

I have wondered, at times, if we have been aided or if our very lives have been preserved through the help of an angel. When our daughter Sally was five, a snow tunnel she made collapsed on her, and she couldn't move or breathe. She said she felt a dog tugging at the legs of her snowpants until she was released from her snowy tomb. And yet, when she was freed, and a few moments later, when we both looked, a dog was nowhere to be seen.

Listen to "The Desire of the Afflicted."

*12.   Psalm 34 is filled with beautiful word pictures. Ask the Lord to widen your imagination. If you could paint, what might you paint to depict each of the following?

A. Psalm 34:5

B. Psalm 34:6

C. Psalm 34:7

D. Psalm 34:8-10

13.   Describe how angels helped those who feared God in the following:
A. Exodus 14:15-20

B. Exodus 23:20-31

C. Daniel 6:19-23

D. Acts 12:6-11

14.   There is only one other psalm that refers to "the angel of the Lord," and it is the next one. In Psalm 34, he surrounds and protects the believer. What does he do in Psalm 35:4-8?

How are the above pictures different from the way angels are usually portrayed today?

15.   What does Jesus tell us about angels and children in Matthew 18:10?

*16. What command is given in Psalm 34:8? Give an example of how you have done this in your own life and how it has impacted you.

*17. What command, promise, and illustration is given in Psalm 34:9-10?

> *Of all the beasts the lion is most powerful and least likely to go hungry. And among the lions . . . young lions are active and successful as hunters. The young lions thus symbolize the essence of self-sufficiency. . . . And yet, as the psalmist demonstrates, it is the self-sufficient predators of the world who would lack, while the God-fearing would have all their needs met.[8]*
> *Peter Craigie*

Day 4: The Eyes of the Lord Are on the Righteous

The hymn closes and the sermon begins in verse 11. The passage we will study today is quoted by Peter in his first letter. Peter's letter is addressed to believers facing persecution, and this particular section from Psalm 34 follows Peter's specific instructions to women. (For an in-depth study of this passage see *A Woman's Journey through 1 Peter*.) There were many women in the early church who placed their trust in Christ before their husbands, and they faced particularly difficult circumstances. Yet Peter wanted to reassure them that the Lord's eyes were on them, and that He heard their cry. He also wanted to remind them of how they should behave when they faced persecution from their husbands or from the unbelieving world in general.

Begin your quiet time by singing along with "The Desire of the Afflicted." Can you sing this now by heart?

18.   Read 1 Peter 3:1-16 in its entirety, and then answer:
      A. "In the same way" in verse 1 refers back to the example of Jesus in 1 Peter 2:21-23. What hope does Peter give the woman who follows in the steps of Jesus? (1 Peter 3:1)

B. What kind of life in a Christian woman is likely to win others? (1 Peter 3:2-4)

C. Sarah was considered an incredibly beautiful woman. We become her "daughters" if we do a number of things. Find them. (v. 6)

D. What phrase is repeated for husbands in 1 Peter 3:7? Implication?

E. How might Psalm 34:12-16 (quoted in 1 Peter 3:10-12) help believers who are facing persecution?

F. Whom should we not fear? Whom should we fear? (1 Peter 3:14)

*19. Read Psalm 34:11-16 carefully and then answer:
    A. How does this "sermon" begin and to whom is it directed?

B. There are six admonitions in verses 13-14. Find them.

C. What contrast is made in verses 15 and 16?

D. How have you seen this contrast elsewhere in psalms we've studied?

20. If you are married to a man "who does not obey the Word," or if you have unbelievers in your family, how might you apply the lessons from today's passages?

Day 5: A Righteous Man May Have Many Troubles

We have trouble believing how much the Lord loves us—especially when we are overwhelmed with trouble. "Broken hearts," Spurgeon writes, "think God far away, when he is really most near to them." (Psalm 34:18) He elaborates,

> "The eyes of the Lord are upon the righteous." . . . They are so dear to him that He cannot take his eyes off them. . . . Their cry he hears at once, even as mother is sure to hear her sick babe.[9]

We often think that trouble means we are unloved. Yet if we look at the Lord's beloved, we see that they have faced many trials and tribulations. In the close of this psalm, we see David, but we can also see Jesus. God ministered to David in the wilderness, and though David received bumps and bruises, God kept his bones from being broken. This is also a Messianic prophecy, for though the bones of the crucified were usually broken, Christ's were not (John 19:32-36).

When life gets difficult, as it surely will, it is helpful to look at Jesus. If He suffered, why shouldn't we? Yet God eventually delivered Christ and exalted Him. We can trust this God to deliver us as well.

Prepare your heart by singing "The Desire of the Afflicted."

Read Psalm 34:17-22.
*21. What promise is given in verse 17? What do you think this means?

David elaborates on verse 17 in verses 18 and 19. The parallelism in the psalms (a thought is repeated in different words) helps us to immerse ourselves and concentrate on God's thoughts.

> That which seems to be unnecessary repetition to us, who are inclined to pray too hurriedly, is actually proper immersion and concentration in prayer.[10]
> Dietrich Bonhoeffer

Sing "The Desire of the Afflicted." As you sing, make it a prayer.

*22. To what two groups of people, according to verse 18, is the Lord particularly near?

> David (Paul) Cho now heads Yoido Full Gospel Church in Seoul, Korea, generally regarded as the largest church in the world today. But as a young man he was a Buddhist, dying of tuberculosis in hopeless poverty. He had heard that "the God of the Christians" helped people, healed people, so where he was he simply asked "their" God to help him. And their God did. He healed this young Korean man.
>
> Do Jesus and his Father hear Buddhists when they call upon them? They hear anyone who calls upon them. "The Lord is near to the brokenhearted, and saves those who are crushed in spirit."[11]
> Dallas Willard

23.   What similar promise do you find in Isaiah 57:15?

24.   Share a time when you experienced the nearness of the Lord, either when you were brokenhearted or truly repentant.

*25. What do you think you will remember about this week's lesson?

Prayer Time

Read each of the following as a springboard for prayer. When there is a silence, read the next passage.

Psalm 34:1-3

Psalm 34:7

Psalm 34:12-14

Psalm 34:18-19

four

Why Are You Downcast, O My Soul?

P raying the psalms has the power to send evil spirits, depression, and anxiety fleeing. After David was secretly anointed as king, King Saul would often call for this young man to play on his harp. King Saul had been abandoned by God and was plagued by an evil spirit—but a transformation occurred in Saul when David came and sang the psalms.

> *Whenever the evil spirit from God came to Saul, David would take the harp and play it with his hand; and Saul would be refreshed and be well, and the evil spirit would depart from him.*
> 1 Samuel 16:23 (NASB)

When you are depressed or discouraged, the same power is available to you. Though we cannot be sure who authored Psalm 42, and will therefore refer to the author as "the psalmist," Charles Spurgeon is convinced it is David.

> *It is so Davidic, it smells of the son of Jesse, it bears the marks of his style and experience in every letter.*[1]

But whether it is David or another psalm writer, listen to how he repeatedly sings to his own soul in Psalm 42, until it finally is released from depression. The song "Why Are You Downcast, O My Soul?" skillfully captures the heart of this psalm through a male voice (representing the psalmist) and a chorus of female voices (representing the soul). Listen to CD track 4 and hear the conversation that goes back and forth between the psalmist and his soul.

Why Are You Downcast, O My Soul?

Why are you downcast, O my soul
Why so disturbed within me
(Repeat)

Put your hope in God
For I will yet praise Him
(Repeat 3 times)

My Savior and my God
(Repeat 2 times)

Danny Chambers
© 1992 Integrity's Praise! Music/BMI
Soloist: Lenny LeBlanc

Warm-Up

Can you remember a time when you were very thirsty? Describe how you felt, your drive, and your feeling when you finally had that thirst quenched.

Day 1: Why We Should Pray the Psalms

Dietrich Bonhoeffer lived during the time of the Nazi control of Germany and took a courageous stand against the Holocaust and Hitler. He was imprisoned and eventually martyred for his faith. In his book *Psalms: The Prayer Book of the Bible*, Bonhoeffer explains the importance of praying through the psalms:

> It is a dangerous error, surely very widespread among Christians, to think that the heart can pray by itself. . . . Prayer does not mean simply to pour out one's heart. It means rather to find the way to God and to speak with him, whether the heart is full or empty. No man can do that by himself. For that he needs Jesus Christ.

> . . . If we wish to pray with confidence and gladness, then the Words of Holy Scripture will have to be the solid basis of our prayer. For here we know that Jesus Christ, the Word of God, teaches us to pray.[2]

How, some may wonder, can the words of Jesus be in the Psalms? Is not David or another psalm writer speaking in the Psalms?

All Scripture is inspired by God, and the Spirit of God speaks through the authors. Some may wonder how Jesus, whom they perceive as being born at Christmas, could be in the Old Testament. Jesus poses this very riddle to the religious leaders.

> Then Jesus presented them with a question. "Why is it," he asked, "that the Messiah is said to be the son of David? For David himself wrote in the book of Psalms:
>
> > 'The Lord said to my Lord,
> > Sit in honor at my right hand
> > Until I humble your enemies,
> > Making them a footstool under your feet.'
>
> Since David called him Lord, how can he be his son at the same time?"
> Luke 20:41-45 (NLT)

The answer to the riddle is that Jesus came after David, yet He came before David as well. In the incarnation, Jesus was David's son, his descendant. But it is vital to remember that Jesus has always existed. He came before David, in fact, He created David. Therefore, David calls the Messiah *Lord*, for He is King David's superior. Bonhoeffer writes,

> In the Psalms of David the promised Christ himself already speaks (Hebrews 2:12; 10:5) or, as may also be indicated, the Holy Spirit. (Hebrews 3:7) The same words which David spoke, therefore, the future Messiah spoke through him. The prayers of David were prayed also by Christ. Or better, Christ himself prayed them through his forerunner David.[3]

The New Testament writers were very familiar with the Psalms, and quote them frequently, as in the sermons in the book of Acts. Jesus prayed the Psalms, and when we follow in His steps, we experience power. They remind us to seek God in all kinds of situations and to trust Him. When we pray the Psalms with our mind and our heart, we connect with God. When we pray Scripture, we know we are praying within the will of God. This is not the "power of positive thinking;" it is the power of God.

Listen to "Why Are You Downcast, O My Soul?" (track 4)

1.   What reasons did you discover for praying the Psalms?

2.   Read 1 Samuel 16 carefully. What verses in this passage help you to understand why the evil spirit may have been driven away when David came to play his harp?

3.   What reason can you find for praying the Psalms from the following?
      A. Ephesians 5:18-19

      B. Colossians 3:16

      C. John 17:17

The above is a quotation from Psalm 119:9. Jesus prayed the Psalms—and we are to follow in His steps.

Day 2: As the Deer Panteth for the Water

I lamented to my twenty-four-year-old daughter that Integrity Music didn't own the rights to "As the Deer" so I wouldn't be able to use it on the CD to go with this book. "It's such a beautiful praise chorus, and so beloved, and it follows Psalm 42:1 perfectly."

"Mom," she said, "if it is any consolation, I need a twenty-year break from 'As the Deer.'"

I laughed. It is true we can sing some of the best praise songs almost to their death. And yet, it is a lovely song—so if you don't need a twenty-year break, and you know it, sing it now, in preparation for the opening of Psalm 42.

4. What stands out to you in your overview reading of this psalm? Why?

5. What word picture is given in Psalm 42:1? What images does it bring to your imagination?

6. In Psalm 42:1-4:
    A. The psalmist compares himself to the deer in verse 1, but to what does he compare God? What do you learn from this part of the word picture?

    B. There is an irony in verse 3a. His soul thirsts for the water of a fresh flowing stream, but instead, what does he receive?

    C. How is the psalmist taunted in verse 3b? And again in verse 10?

    D. What the psalmist longs for is the face of God—not His comforts, or His gifts—but His countenance. He wants to be intimate with God, to know His nearness, His fellowship. A fugitive, he is cut off from worship, so he now consoles himself, in verse 4, with memory. What does he recall?

C.S. Lewis comments on the longing we see in the above passage, saying that it shows a great "appetite" for God, described in terms of a physical thirst. Lewis suggests that "appetite for God" may better describe what we need in our lives than the phrase "love for God," for:

"The love of God" too easily suggests the word "spiritual" in all those negative or restrictive senses which it has unhappily acquired.[4]

7.   Do you have an "appetite" for God? When you wake up, do you long to rush into His arms? Do you dialogue with Him throughout the day? Are you hungry to have Him teach you from His Word? Describe your appetite.

Sing along with "Why Art Thou Downcast, O My Soul?"

Day 3: Why So Disturbed Within Me?

As I sobbed in the night, feeling the pain of a relationship with a family member that has been extremely difficult, my husband put his arms around me. He said, "Do you think the Lord allows thorns in order to keep us close to Him?"

"Perhaps," I said. I certainly know all pain has the potential of bringing us closer to Him. If we respond correctly, it has the potential of prompting us to examine our lives for sin and cling to the Lord in faith, trusting His sovereignty.

The psalmist has to fight off depression, as it sweeps over him like billows of waves. The theme of water is throughout Psalm 42. As he begins to preach to his soul, he is temporarily uplifted. But then the wells of depression sweep over him again, like the roar of a waterfall. "Deep calls to deep," he laments. Taunting voices above and below join together in a chorus against him. He sinks down, as waves of depression sweep over him.

To prepare your heart, listen to "Why Are You Downcast, O My Soul?" Can you sing the lyrics by heart?

*8.   Meditate on Psalm 42:5-7.
    A. What questions does the psalmist ask of his soul in verse 5a?

    B. What two solutions does the psalmist give in verse 5b?

Think it not enough to silence thy heart from quarrelling with God, but leave not till thou canst bring it sweetly to rely on God. Holy David drove it thus far; he did not only chide his soul for being disquieted, but he charges it to trust in God.[5]
William Gurnall (1617-1679)

    C. In verse 6, the psalmist remembers various times when he was close to the Lord. Remembering such times can help us fight discouragement. List a few times and places when you were close to God.

    D. What word pictures for his depression does the psalmist give in verse 7?

*9.   What can you learn from this psalm about overcoming depression and regaining the countenance of God? What should you do? What shouldn't you do?

*10.   Choose an area in your life where you have been downcast. Follow the psalmist's example by asking your soul *why* you are downcast. Make a list of the things that contribute to your discouragement. Then look at each one and consider how knowing and trusting God might help you respond.

<u>Contributions to discouragement</u>   <u>Reasons to trust God</u>

*11.   God responds in verse 8a and then the psalmist responds to God in 8b and 8c. Find all three parts of this cyclical process.

When the distractions of my medical practice are over for the day, I reflect on how God's lovingkindness flowed to me during the hours past. In the still hours of the night, I respond with praise to the Lord. And then, I respond with prayer, asking for help with the problems of the coming day, for grace, for forgiveness of my sins.[6]

Dr. Steve Brestin

12.   In Lamentations 3:19-33, what similar themes do you find as in this psalm?

Sing along with "Why Art Thou Downcast, O My Soul?"

Day 4: Put Your Hope in God!

David's determination to trust God reminds me of the word picture in Psalm 131, one that women who have mothered babies and small children may particularly appreciate. David compares the person who is humbled and is trusting God with the child who has been weaned. In biblical days, weaning took place much later than it does today and it was often a battle. The child fretted and fussed until he learned to be content with the cup instead of the breast. Today many mothers, particularly in the western world, wean from the breast before the child is a year old, and then the child continues to use a bottle or pacifier until he is two or even three. Whether the weaning is from the breast, bottle, or pacifier, there is sometimes a battle. I remember how I delayed weaning our firstborn from the pacifier, because I knew it would be hard for him (and me!). When he turned three, I tried reasoning with him, saying, "J.R., big boys don't use pacifiers."

Wide-eyed and confused, talking with the plug in his mouth, he said: "But I'm a big boy—and I use a pacifier."

Then I bribed him with a red fire engine, for which he eagerly traded. But when he realized the pacifier was truly, truly gone, there were many tears.

Eventually, one day, he was content. He was weaned.

From what do we need to be weaned? Our pride. Our self-sufficiency. From anything more important to us than God. There may be a painful time when we are learning to do without overeating, or soap operas, or a consuming career . . . but finally, we are content, and God has moved in and filled that space with peace and joy. Only God can give us lasting contentment.

13.   Meditate on Psalm 131.
      A. What is David not doing in verse 1? What are one or two ways in which you follow (or need to follow) his example?

      B. What is David doing in verse 2a that reminds you of the chorus of "Why Are You Downcast, O My Soul?"

      C. What does the word picture in verse 2 mean to you?

D. What is the secret of lasting peace and contentment according to verse 3?

A soul weaned from the world still pants as much as ever for food and happiness, but it no longer seeks them in worldly things, or desires to do so.[7]
Charles Bradley (1836)

14.   From what do you need to be weaned?

Returning to Psalm 42, we find David again quieting his soul. Spurgeon says that when the spasm of despondency returns, then David takes down his harp again, making the evil spirit flee.[8]

Sing "Why Are You Downcast, O My Soul?" in your personal quiet time.

15.   Meditate on Psalm 42:9-11.
   A. One of the secrets of a person who practices the presence of God is that she continually dialogues with God. What question does David ask of God in verse 9?

   B. Some have said we only need to pray something once, and then simply trust God. But David's model is different in this psalm, according to verses 5 and 11. What do you learn from this that you could apply to an area in which you are struggling?

Day 5: For I Will Yet Praise Him, My Savior and My God
Charles Spurgeon didn't think we should have other people or instruments do our praising for us in church. He wrote, "We might as well pray by machinery as praise by it."[9]

Author and speaker Lyndsey O'Connor tells how the Lord taught her this lesson. One day she was feeling low and discouraged. She knows, scripturally, that one of the sacrifices that delights the Lord is our praise. So, though she didn't feel like it, she turned on praise music as she was doing the dishes. She listened to the choir sing praise songs, but her spirit did not lift.

"Lord," she said, "I don't feel any better."

In her heart, the Lord responded immediately: "That's *their* praise. Where's *yours*?"

Somewhat begrudgingly, Lyndsey began to sing along. As she sang, she began to think about the lyrics and focus on the Lord. By the time three or four songs had passed, her soul was quieted, and the sun had peeked out from the clouds.[10]

Prepare your heart by singing "Why Are You Downcast, O My Soul?"

16. Do you sing Scripture songs, praise choruses, and hymns as you go about your day? When during the day do you have opportunities to do this?

17. Read Psalm 43, a companion to Psalm 42.
   A. What argument does David give to God in Psalm 43:1-2?

   B. David flees again to God. What is his desire, as seen in Psalm 43:3-4?

   C. What refrain from Psalm 42 is repeated in Psalm 43:5?

18.   Consider how an Old Testament prophet handled the severe conditions found in the Book of Habakkuk. Read Habakkuk 3:17-19.

   A. Describe the circumstances in which Habakkuk is determined to praise the Lord.

   B. Describe the source of Habakkuk's joy.

Read Psalm 42 and 43 again.

*19. What do you think you will remember from this week's lesson? How will you apply it to your life?

Prayer Time

Use the following verses from Psalm 42 as your springboard for prayer:

Psalm 42:1

Psalm 42:5

Psalm 42:6

Five

Whiter Than Snow

True repentance is evidenced by *brokenness*. Many times, I've seen this occur vividly at women's seminars. God's truth is spoken, and His light falls, revealing the crimson stain of a hidden sin—a betrayal, a bitterness that has been nurtured, a sexual sin, an abortion. The Spirit is moving, convicting . . . and when the invitation is given, women make their way to the front. They kneel, weeping. Each wonders, as she sees the ugliness of her own sin: *Can a holy God truly forgive* me? *Will He truly make* me *whiter than snow?*

Yes, oh, yes. He has the power to make us whiter than the pure and pristine snow that falls upon the mountains and blankets the meadows.

This is the beauty and the power of Psalm 51. Of the seven penitential psalms, Psalm 51 is the best known. It was written after David had committed adultery with Bathsheba and, in an attempted cover up, had her husband murdered. If God can forgive a king whom He had so blessed of such grievous sins, then He can forgive anyone. Of course God can forgive anyone He chooses to forgive, but David's complete repentance provides an important model for us.

From the world's point of view, David had it all—good looks, talent, power, wealth, and any woman he wanted. Yet when the prophet Nathan came to him and confronted him about his sin, David was crushed, overwhelmed with grief. For what David wanted most in life was fellowship with God. He realized he had grieved the One who meant everything to him. He finally admits he has lost the sweet countenance of the Lord's face. Now nothing else matters, nothing else can recompense for what David has lost—his sin is ever before him. He feels like the leper, covered with oozing sores. How can anything else possibly bring joy while he feels like this?

If only we would see sin as seriously as David did. Surely the world does not. When my husband and I first became believers in Christ, we were overwhelmed with gratitude for what He had done for us. When our eyes were finally opened to the depravity of our sin we felt so dirty, so afraid, so helpless. And then! So cleansed, so freed, so empowered.

We found a Christmas card that perfectly portrayed our joy in being forgiven. It was a painting of a bright red cardinal against a backdrop of sparkling snow. Underneath was the promise:

> *Though your sins are like scarlet*
> *They shall be as white as snow*
> > Isaiah 1:18

How naïve we were not to have anticipated the reaction from our many unbelieving friends! They were deeply offended. Our sins as scarlet? *Were the Brestins implying that they were sinful? Not only that, that their sins were as scarlet?* What was now so obvious to us, because we had been given a glimpse of the awesome holiness of God and therefore, of our own wretchedness, was deeply offensive to those still in darkness.

Yet even the believer commonly fails to see sin as God does. John Calvin wrote,

> *The more easily satisfied we are under our sins, the more do we provoke God to punish them with severity.*[1]

We need to live in a state of perpetual repentance, realizing that our sins, even the ones we may minimize (gossip, overeating, laziness . . .) make God weep and rob us of power and peace. We need a heart like David's, a heart that wants to be excised of its evil, a heart that longs to be restored to the joy of our salvation.

Listen to "Whiter Than Snow" on track 5. Feel the emotion. Meditate on the lyrics.

Whiter Than Snow

*For I acknowledge my transgressions
And my sin is always before me
Against You, You only
Have I sinned
And done this evil in Your sight
That You may be found just when You speak
And blameless when You judge*

*Purge me with hyssop
And I shall be clean
Wash me and I shall be
Whiter than snow
(Repeat)*

Bob Ayala
© 1994 Integrity's Hosanna! Music/ASCAP
Soloist: Greg Barnhill

Warm-Up

When you were a little girl and got a splinter, what do you remember about how you felt about its removal?

Day 1: The Fall

In his book *Temptation*, Dietrich Bonhoeffer says,

> *In our members there is a slumbering inclination toward desire, which is both sudden and fierce . . . the flesh burns and is in flames. . . . It makes no difference whether it is sexual desire, or ambition, or . . . desire for revenge. . . . At this moment God is quite unreal to us.*[2]

You may not be tempted by adultery, as David was—but there is something. And at that moment, God becomes quite unreal to you.

I can identify with this. All of my life I have struggled with overeating. In the morning, I set my face like flint, but many times, by evening, I rationalize, and "God becomes unreal to me" so that I can indulge my flesh.

I have experienced a measure of victory in this battle as my love for God and the joy of fellowship with Him has grown. For now, when I sin, I grieve as much for the loss of God's countenance as for the gain shown on my bathroom scale. I am learning more and more that nothing, absolutely nothing, is worth shutting out the rays of His light.

1.   What stood out to you from the introduction?

2.   Read 2 Samuel 11 as an overview. Though this is a familiar story, ask the Lord to show you something relevant for your life. What stood out to you and why?

3.   Do you have an area where you like to shut God out so that you can do what you want to do? If so, explain how you are deceiving yourself.

4.   In Psalm 32:3-4, what word pictures does David give to describe how he felt before true repentance?

Read Psalm 51 in its entirety.
5.   What does God impress upon your heart in this initial reading?

Listen to "Whiter Than Snow" and begin to learn the lyrics.

Day 2: For I Acknowledge My Transgression
When our children were little and they would get a splinter, sometimes they would hide it or deny it or pretend that they had gotten it out. Anything but face the tweezers, the needle, the probing of the tender flesh!

I understand. I've done the same thing with the splinters of sin in my life. But then the infection begins, and the throbbing becomes unbearable. When I finally hold out my hand, admit my splinter, and say, "Please be gentle with me, Lord, but do what You must to get it all out," He then excises that long, dark splinter, and yes, it hurts a great deal! But then He washes me tenderly, applies salve, and the healing can truly begin.

True repentance is rare. What we practice, more often, is pseudo-repentance. We hold back part of the truth, defend ourselves, and focus the blame on others. There is not a broken heart. There is not changed behavior. But in true repentance,

> *you may cry, you may laugh out loud. . . . But you won't be defensive or angry or proud or bitter. A contrite heart makes no demands and has no expectations. Broken and humble people are simply grateful to be alive.*[3]
> Charles Swindoll

Nathan was enormously skillful in breaking down David's natural defenses. Why did God wait so long to send Nathan? Perhaps to allow David to experience the pain of hiding that long ugly splinter. God filled Nathan's mouth with His words and sent him to David at exactly the right time.

Read 2 Samuel 12:1-25.

6.   Meditate on Nathan's confrontation of David in 2 Samuel 12:1-14:
A. How do you think David might have responded if Nathan had confronted him directly instead of using a parable? Why?

B. Describe how David felt in verse 5 and the sentence that he thought should be carried out.

C. What statement did Nathan make in verse 7? Why do you think Nathan was so courageous?

D. David sat silently as Nathan listed the reasons for God's anger and the consequences that would come to David as a result of his sin. Describe each in verses 8-12.

E. Describe David's response. (2 Samuel 12:13 and also Psalm 51:3)

F. Despite the many consequences, there is still mercy from God. What is it, according to 2 Samuel 12:13b?

G. What did Nathan say would happen to the child? (v. 14)

Joseph Excell, of the *Pulpit Commentary*, explains,

> *Jehovah's enemies are not the heathen, but Israelitish unbelievers, who would scoff at all religion when one in David's position fell into terrible open sin. But the death of the adulterous offspring of David and Bathsheba would prove to these irreligious men that Jehovah's righteous rule could reach and punish the king himself, and would thus vindicate his justice from their reproach.*[4]

7. Describe some consequences you have had to face as a result of sin and how these consequences were in line with God's holiness and justice.

In 2 Samuel 12:15-25 we see David praying. As Psalm 51 shows us, this was a time of true repentance, of *penitence* for his sin. But he also prayed for the child. It is not wrong to pray for mercy, it is not wrong, even, to ask to be spared the consequences for our sins. Sometimes God will do that. But if He does not, we must, as David models here, accept it when God chooses to instead give justice.

8.   From 2 Samuel 12:15-25:
   A. Describe David's behavior after the child became ill. (vv. 16-17)

   B. What fear did the servants have? (vv. 18-19)

I think of David's situation when I hear people who have been caught in sin complain that others are talking about it—as if the real problem is everyone else's lack of respect for their privacy. My motto on this is "Don't assume you have a greater right to privacy than King David!" The corollary is, "Don't do it, if you don't want people to talk about it." [5]
Dorian Coover-Cox

   C. How did David's behavior stun the servants? (vv. 20-21)

David's determination to worship showed that he was truly repentant. David was demonstrating to all that he accepted God's justice.

Have you ever returned to the Lord in worship after a painful loss that you believe He could have stopped? If so, you may view your return to worship as one of the most difficult and painful experiences of life. I suspect David would concur, but his return restored his sanity. His rediscovered relationship with God became the pillar to hold him up through the painful repercussions of his sins. [6]
Beth Moore

   D. What phrase in verse 22 shows David's confidence that he and his child will be reunited in heaven? How might this comfort bereaved parents?

E. How does God then show mercy to David and Bathsheba? (vv. 24-25)

Listen to "Whiter Than Snow." Sing with it.

Day 3: Against You, You Only, Have I Sinned

Today we move into the beloved Psalm 51, which some have called the brightest gem of the whole book. It is certainly the fullest confession of sin anywhere in Scripture. We also will consider the most controversial verse in the whole psalm:

> *Against You, You only, have I sinned*
> Psalm 51:4a

What does David mean? He sinned against his whole kingdom, against Bathsheba, against Bathsheba's husband, whom he murdered in an attempt to cover his sin, against his children, and against God.

Many scholars have attempted an explanation of this verse. The one I repeatedly see that makes sense is that David is taking poetic license here. It isn't that he doesn't realize that he has sinned against many people. It is that God now looms above him as so awesome and so holy that David can see no one else. David realizes how evil he is compared to his holy God and how he has always been evil and will always be evil. The closer we grow to God, the more conscious we become of displeasing God, until we say, with David, *You, dear Lord, You are the One I have hurt the most . . . and You are the only One I can think about.*

In *My Utmost for His Highest*, Oswald Chambers writes,

> *Very few of us know anything about conviction of sin. We know the experience of being disturbed because we have done wrong things. But conviction of sin by the Holy Spirit blots out every relationship on earth and makes us aware of only one—"Against You, You only, have I sinned." (Psalm 51:4)*[7]

Sing "Whiter Than Snow" to prepare your heart.

9.   Meditate on Psalm 51:1-6.

A. On what grounds does David hope for mercy? (v. 1)

B. David's request is repeated three times in verses 1b and 2. List the three verbs and what the repetition tells you.

He desires to be rid of the whole mass of his filthiness. . . . "Lord, if washing will not do, try some other process; if water avails not, let fire, let anything be tried, that I may but be purified."[8]
                      Charles Spurgeon

C. How heavily does David's sin weigh on him according to verse 3? Have you ever felt that way? When?

D. How do you interpret verse 4a?

E. When we experience consequences as a result of our sin, what does it reveal about the character of God according to verse 4b?

F. Why might it have been important that the world watching David saw that he had to suffer consequences for adultery and murder? (Psalm 51:4b)

G. How long has David been sinful according to verse 5?

10. How is Psalm 51:5 corroborated by Psalm 58:3? By Job 14:4?

When I was the mother of two little boys, I was trying to follow the contemporary belief that I should not spank my children. It wasn't working. Then I heard a message by pastor and author Larry Christenson that changed my approach. He told me when to spank (for willful disobedience) and how (never in anger, but with a spirit of regret, in obedience to God, to help that child obey and honor God) and why. He explained the world believes man is innately good, so they think that as soon as the child sees the reason for his wrong, he will turn around. Christenson disagreed, on the basis of Scripture. Because man is bent on evil from birth, a child needs loving but firm discipline in order to choose the right path. When they are young, they can be molded, like soft clay on the potter's wheel. But if neglected, they will harden into distorted and ugly shapes. Today we are grateful, that because of God's mercy, our sons are men who love and honor God.

> *Discipline your son in his early years while there is hope. If you don't you will ruin his life.*
> *Proverbs 19:18 (TLB)*

11. If you have had success in raising godly children, share a sentence about what you did to help your children obey and honor you and, eventually, God.

12. From each of us God desires much more than outward obedience, though that is the beginning. What is He after, according to Psalm 51:6?

> *What you're after is truth from the inside out.*
> *Enter me, then; conceive a new, true life.*
> *Psalm 51:6 (TM)*

Day 4: Purge Me with Hyssop

Hyssop is a branch that was dipped in the blood of the sacrifice and used for sprinkling. Israelites understood the powerful ritual. The first mention is in the Passover, when the Lord instructed them, through Moses,

> *Go at once and select the animals for your families and slaughter the Passover lamb. Take a bunch of hyssop, dip it into the blood in the basin and put some of the blood on the top and on both sides of the doorframe.*
> *Exodus 12:21b-22a*

This was a foreshadowing of Christ, our Passover Lamb. It is only through His blood that we can be protected from God's righteous wrath and that we can be cleansed from the deep stain in our souls. *Purge me with hyssop*, David pleads, *and I shall be clean.*

Sing "Whiter Than Snow" along with your Integrity CD.

13.   Describe the great need in each of the following incidents. Put yourself in their place; imagine how you would feel if you were the one in need of the blood sprinkled with the hyssop.
    A. Exodus 12:21-24

    B. Leviticus 14:1-7

I don't like to think about the worst things I have done wrong. I identify with David's grief when he said, *My sin is ever before me.* Things I did in my youth, ways I hurt my beloved parents, can still make me weep, though I know I have been cleansed. And how thankful I am for the power of the blood and its ability to make me *whiter than snow.* I also realize it is an act of faith to believe that Christ's blood is sufficient and to trust that cleansing power.

14.   How can the following passages increase your confidence in God's power to cleanse from any sin? What promise is given?
   A. Isaiah 1:18

   B. Hebrews 9:13-14

   C. 1 John 1:7-9

Do you believe that God has the power to cleanse you from every sin, no matter how heinous? Will you reject Satan's lies that God will not forgive you for sexual immorality, an abortion, or a betrayal? Will you claim the promise of God that you can be whiter than snow? Will you go and sin no more?

15.   What word picture is given to describe the change in a sinner who is trusting the cleansing power of God in Psalm 51:8?

This line is perhaps my favorite in Psalm 51. . . . God sometimes uses circumstances and discipline to figuratively break our legs from continuing on the path of sin. Only the repentant know what it's like to dance with joy and gladness on broken legs![9]
                                    Beth Moore

Day 5: Create in Me a Clean Heart, O God

Recently I visited a woman who has been a mentor to me. I told her, "I want to be like you—I want to consistently react to people like you do, with purity of heart and with great compassion."

She rolled her eyes. "I don't always, Dee," she said. Then she told me that right now she was having to daily interact with one who had hurt her deeply. "Purity is a very high calling," she sighed. She told me that when she wakes up, and several times throughout the day, she pleads,

> Create in me a clean heart, O God;
> and renew a right spirit within me
> Psalm 51:10 (KJV)

If you know the familiar praise chorus based on Psalm 51:10-12, sing it now, to prepare your heart. Then read Psalm 51:10-19.

16. List the requests David makes of God in Psalm 51:10-12.

17. When the above is true, what follows, according to verse 13? Explain.

18. What does God *not* delight in? What does He delight in?

Personal Prayer Time
Confess any sin that weighs on your heart. Write it down and determine to turn completely from it. Then take a match to that piece of paper and burn it. As far as the east is from the west, so has God removed your transgressions.

*19. What do you think you will remember from this week's lesson? How will you apply it to your life?

Prayer Time
Pray through Psalm 51:10-13, a verse at a time, followed by conversational prayer. Close by singing "Whiter Than Snow" together.

Six

Give Thanks

Our daughter-in-law Julie has made a wonderful memory album, filled with photos and stories about God's tender mercies to her and her family. She has called it *The Against Forgetting Album*. One page records how she was born with a hole in her heart and of how God answered her parents' prayers and brought her safely through the surgery. Another tells the story of how God brought our son into her life. She chronicles God's nearness to them in the sorrow of the miscarriages of their first two babies. This is followed by joyful pages concerning the births of their four children, accompanied by stories of answered prayers, tender mercies, and evidence after evidence that we belong to a God who bends down and answers prayer.

One of the psalms we will study this week, Psalm 78, could be called "The Against Forgetting Psalm." It grieves God when, despite His great goodness to us, we neither thank Him nor remember what He has done for us. Psalm 78 records many of God's wonderful acts for the Israelites, and yet:

> *They forgot what he had done,*
> *The wonders he had shown them. . . .*
>
> *They spoke against God, saying,*
> *"Can God spread a table in the desert?*
> *When he struck the rock, water gushed out,*
> *And streams flowed abundantly.*
> *But can he also give us food?*
> *Can he supply meat for his people?"*
> *Psalm 78:11, 19-20*

Our hearts should be filled with gratitude and humility all the day long. This is beautifully expressed in the song "Give Thanks." This week we will study three psalms on the importance of thankfulness for God's tender mercies.

Listen to "Give Thanks" on track 6.

Give Thanks

Give thanks with a grateful heart
Give thanks to the Holy One
Give thanks because He's given
Jesus Christ His Son
(Repeat)

And now let the weak say I am strong
Let the poor say I am rich
Because of what the Lord has done for us
(Repeat)

Henry Smith
© 1978 Integrity's Hosanna! Music/ASCAP
Soloist: Don Moen

Warm-Up

Every Thanksgiving our family goes around the table with the following question: "What is one thing you are thankful for that you could not have been thankful for last year?" Do it now, but limit yourself to one breath.

Day One: Give Thanks

The psalm we are studying today, Psalm 75, is reminiscent of Hannah's song of praise and Mary's Magnificat. The world in which they lived was oppressive of those in humble circumstances. Women were second-class citizens. Barren women were shamed. Poor people were oppressed. But God turned the tables. Both of these devout women experienced great favor from God. Hannah conceived Samuel, who would become a mighty prophet. Mary was chosen to be the mother of the Christ. The weak were made strong. The poor were made rich. And each of these women returned to sing a song of thanksgiving to the Lord.

*1.   What stood out to you from the introduction to this chapter?

Hannah had suffered persecution from her husband's other wife, who taunted her because she was barren. Hannah poured out her heart to God, and He answered, giving her Samuel.

2.   In Hannah's song of praise in 1 Samuel 2:1-10, what are the prevailing themes?

3.   Can you think of a situation in which you were being treated unfairly, but instead of taking matters into your own hands, you committed your case to God and He answered? If so, share something about it briefly, with thanksgiving.

Read Psalm 75.
4.   In Psalm 75:
   A. For what does the psalmist give thanks in verse 1? What does this mean?

   B. What theme do you see in verses 4-7?

   C. Rams, bucks, and many other animals use their horns in battle to establish dominance. Men wore helmets with horns (and this is also the origin of crowns) to represent dominance. What does the psalmist say about horns in verses 4 and 10?

D. What does the word picture in verse 8 mean? (cf. Jeremiah 25:15)

Hannah sang in 1 Samuel 2:1a and 8a:
My heart rejoices in the LORD . . .
He raises the poor from the dust and lifts the needy from the ash heap.

Mary sang in Luke 1:46 and 1:52:
My soul glorifies the Lord . . .
He has brought down rulers from their thrones but has lifted up the humble.

The psalmist sang in Psalm 75:1 and 75:7:
We give thanks to you, O God . . .
He brings one down, he exalts another.

Sometimes those who have been given power abuse it, despite God's severe warnings against this. But there is a power greater. Remember how Jesus did not take matters into His own hands but committed His case to the One who judges justly (1 Peter 2:23). Likewise, see how frequently David prays for justice, all the while remembering how God has acted in the past.

5.   Are you facing a situation right now where you are being treated unfairly or where you are facing a controlling spirit? Write your prayer here and then be alert for the answer, remembering to respond with a thankful heart.

Day Two: That the Next Generation May Know

Psalm 78 is one of several psalms recounting Israel's history, pleading with God's people to *remember* God's merciful and mighty acts toward them. They are to tell these deeds to their children, so that they will in turn tell their children.

Today so many of our children do not know the great hymns of the faith, even the Christmas carols. They do not know the Bible stories, even the Easter story. And if they do know, often they do not understand the meaning. Psalm 78 talks about understanding *the hidden things*. If we pass down the stories without also passing down the central meaning, it is like passing down the husks of corn without the golden fruit. Because the story without the meaning is not satisfying, soon even it will not be passed down. Charles Spurgeon writes, "What is not understood will soon be forgotten."[1]

Read the whole psalm as if it is a story. You may want to use an easy to read paraphrase, such as *The Living Bible* or *The Message.*

6.   What would you say is the key lesson of Psalm 78? Find a verse that articulates this key lesson in a nutshell.

How vital it is to see ourselves in the Israelites, to see how easily we grumble, how easily we forget God's goodness, and how slow we are to find ways to pass on His mercies to the next generation!

7.   Choose a Bible story (such as David and Goliath or Christ's resurrection) and articulate the central meaning, which is often not difficult, but still needs to be articulated, especially to a child. How would you pass on the story you have chosen to a child, showing her what it has to do with her?

8.   In Psalm 78:1-8:
   A. What does the psalmist earnestly desire to share with God's people according to verses 2-4?

   B. With what responsibility are we charged, according to verses 4-6?

C. As a mother, grandmother, aunt, or mentor, how are you doing this?

D. In verses 5-8 find several reasons for passing on to the next generation the truths of what God has done.

Sing "Give Thanks" in your personal quiet time.

Day Three: Against Forgetting

How vital it is that we find ways to remember God's mighty acts, not only for the sake of the next generation, but because thankfulness, or the lack of it, profoundly impacts our own hearts, our own faith.

Sing "Give Thanks" to prepare your heart.

9.   What are some of the mighty acts of God, according to Psalm 78:9-16, that the Israelites forgot?

10.   How did their forgetfulness concerning God's goodness to them impact their hearts? (Psalm 78:17-20)

11.   What is the central meaning and application of the above story? How might you apply it to your life?

12.   There is a pattern in Psalm 78. Summarize each step in a few words.

A. Psalm 78:11

B. Psalm 78:17-20

C. Psalm 78:21-22

D. Psalm 78:34-35

E. Psalm 78:36-37

F. Psalm 78:38-39

"As a Father Has Compassion" (track 8) sings about the last part of this pattern. Listen to it now in your personal quiet time.

13.   List a few of the ways God's goodness is evidenced in Scripture. Then list a few ways He has been good to you in the last year that you do not want to forget. Do you keep a journal?

14.   When you think about the trials you may be facing right now, how might the past goodness of God help you to face them with faith? Be specific.

Day Four: I Love the Lord, for He Bent down and Listened
What a beautiful picture Psalm 116 gives us. An awesome God bends down and listens to the humble cry of His child. As He bent down when Hannah cried to Him to be delivered from her barrenness, as He bent down when the Israelites

cried to Him to be delivered from their bondage, so He bends down when we humbly cry to Him. His mercy extends from generation to generation to those who fear Him.

Twelve years ago, my husband, who is a surgeon, had to have surgery on his *own* wrist. We didn't know if he would be able to continue afterward as a surgeon. Experienced surgeons were hesitant to operate on him. Then one of his partners, a dear brother in the Lord, said he would do it, trusting the Lord would be with him. The night before the surgery, all of his partners and their wives met with us to pray.

The surgery was a great success. Steve's wrist was stronger than it ever had been. He has continued his career as a gifted back surgeon. The wife of one of his partners sent me a card, in which she wrote,

> *I love the Lord because he hears my prayers and answers them. Because he bends down and listens, I will pray as long as I breathe!*
> *Psalm 116:1-2 (TLB)*

15.   List one answer to prayer in your life, for which you will not forget to be thankful.

In your quiet time, sing "Give Thanks" with the recording.

Read Psalm 116.
16.   What stands out to you in an overview reading of this psalm?

17.   Meditate on Psalm 116:1-6.
     A. Some say that it is wrong to love God because of what He can do for us, but we should simply love Him for who He is. What contrast do you see in verse 1? Comment.

B. The psalmist prays with his voice (v. 1). Do you pray out loud in your personal prayer time? What advantages can you see for this over silent prayer?

C. What impact does answered prayer have upon the psalmist? (v. 2)

D. What word pictures recall his great need?

E. How can you see the Israelites in this passage? David? Christ?

F. What did the psalmist learn about the Lord from this experience? (vv. 5-6)

Sing "Shout to the Lord" (track 1) to close your quiet time.

Day Five: How Can I Repay the Lord?

We will continue our study of Psalm 116 today. Not only should we give thanks to God, but also we should tell others what God has done for us. Derek Kidner writes,

> There is an infectious delight and touching gratitude about this psalm, the personal tribute of a man whose prayer has found an overwhelming answer. He has come now to the temple to tell the whole assembly what has happened, and to offer God what he had vowed to Him in his extremity.[2]

When God has been good to us, we should tell others. In Psalm 116, we see one clear way to do this, whether we are telling our story of salvation or another story of deliverance:

    A. Where we were (Psalm 116:3)
    B. What we did (Psalm 116:4)
    C. What we learned about the Lord (Psalm 116:5-6)

18.   Apply the above ABCs to telling your story of deliverance. Choose either your story of salvation or another story of when you were in trouble, cried to the Lord, and were delivered. (Hear from one or two in your group, and ask them to be brief. You could also *all* share another time over a special extra lunch meeting.)
    A. What was your situation?

    B. What did you do?

    C. What did you learn about the Lord?

In your quiet time, sing "Give Thanks" and "Why Are You Downcast, O My Soul?"

19.   The psalmist has been upset by his troubles, but now, as David did in Psalm 42, he talks to his soul, commanding it to return to its rest in God. What exactly does he say, and what reasons does he give? (Psalm 116:7-8)

The psalmist asks,
    How can I repay the LORD for all his goodness to me?
             Psalm 116:12

20. How does he then answer the question in:
   A. vv. 13 and 14

The cup of salvation suggests God's gift to man. . . . As the opposite of the "foaming cup" of wrath which we deserve (cf. 75:8), and as something freely offered, it displays the very pattern of the gospel. Man is the suppliant (cf. 13b with 1, 2) and the recipient, before he has anything to give. His only gifts are debts of gratitude. (v. 14)[3]
Derek Kidner

B. vv. 17-19

The people had gathered for a festival. Amidst the communal worship . . . individuals had opportunity to bring thank offerings and to accompany their sacrificial worship with words of testimony and praise for answered prayer.[4]
Leslie C. Allen

Prayer Time

As time permits, gather in circles of four or five and have a time of testimony and thanksgiving for God's tender mercies to you. Read the following verses and then allow a few women to briefly share their testimony of gratitude.

Deliverance from trouble (Psalm 34:4-7)

Forgiveness for sin (Psalm 51:7)

Wonderful deeds to you (Psalm 75:1)

Deliverance from death, tears, stumbling (Psalm 116:8)

Blessings of harmony with brothers and sisters (Psalm 133)

Close by singing "Give Thanks" together.

Seven

Under the Shadow of Your Wings

harles Spurgeon had scarcely begun his ministry in London, in 1854, when the cholera struck:

Family after family summoned me to the bedside of the smitten, and almost every day I was called to visit the grave. . . . I became weary in body and sick at heart. My friends seemed falling one by one and I felt or fancied that I was sickening like those around me.

Families and shopkeepers were posting the alarming sign everywhere:

CHOLERA!

Spurgeon recalled his experience in seeing a very different posting:

As God would have it, I was returning mournfully home from a funeral, when my curiosity led me to read a paper which was wafered up in a shoemaker's window in the Dover Road. In a good bold handwriting were these words:

**Because thou hast made the Lord,
which is my refuge, even the most High,
thy habitation, there shall no evil befall thee,
neither shall any plague come nigh thy dwelling
Psalm 91:9-10**

The effect upon my heart was immediate. Faith appropriated the passage . . . I went on my visitation of the dying in a calm and peaceful spirit; I felt no fear of evil, and I suffered no harm. The providence which moved the tradesman to place those verses in his window I gratefully acknowledge, and in the remembrance of its marvelous power I adore the Lord my God.[1]

You may be thinking, *Wait a minute. Are you saying that no trouble will come to the one who stays very close to the Lord?*

No. God may deliver you from trouble, as He did for the psalmist who wrote Psalm 91. But there are other times when the psalmist was not delivered in the manner he hoped to be delivered. (Remember Psalm 22, for example.) There are times when God seems silent, and psalms are recorded for those circumstances as well. For example, in Psalm 44, the psalmist says that they face death all day long and he cries:

Awake, O Lord! Why do you sleep?
Rouse yourself! Do not reject us forever.
Why do you hide your face
and forget our misery and oppression?
                          Psalm 44:23-24

God's deliverance may look different than the deliverance we hope, in our limited perspective, will be forthcoming. But God is sovereign, good, and concerned about our best. Though the believer may suffer, and even die, no evil will ultimately overcome her. God's peace can surround her and uphold her. In the midst of the most fearful circumstances, she can know the presence of God.

Different psalms are written for different occasions. In the circumstance of Psalm 91, the psalmist cried and the Lord delivered him from trouble. And though deliverance always depends on God's mercy, it is also noteworthy to look at the psalmist's model of dwelling in the secret place of the Most High, of staying under the shadow of His wings. When you are convinced that God is trustworthy, and you are therefore loyal to your King, you are under His shadow, and no matter what happens to you, whether it is the kind of deliverance you hoped for or not, it is for good.

Listen to "Under the Shadow," track 7, on your CD.

Under the Shadow

Under the shadow of Your wings
I will find a hiding place
You are my refuge
A fortress in whom I can trust

Under the shadow of Your wings
I will find a hiding place
You are my refuge
My God in whom I trust

You are my strength
And my shield, O God
I run to You and I find help

Under the shadow
Of Your wings will I abide
And in Your loving arms I will hide

Kent Henry and John Stevenson
© 1988 Integrity's Hosanna! Music/ASCAP & Integrity's Praise! Music/BMI
Soloist: Kelly Willard

Warm-Up

Think about a time when you were in the midst of a fearful experience and experienced the Lord's comfort. Share, in one breath, how He comforted you.

Day 1: A Psalm for Danger

Psalm 91 is a psalm for danger. Many believe it was written by Moses, inspired by his remembrance of how God protected the Israelites who stayed close to Him. The plagues brought their Egyptian enemies low, in fact, the sea swallowed them up, but the Israelites were rescued.

You will not fear the terror of night,
nor the arrow that flies by day,
nor the pestilence that stalks in the darkness,
nor the plague that destroys at midday.
A thousand may fall at your side,
ten thousand at your right hand,
but it will not come near you

Psalm 91:5-6

Others find the language reminiscent of David and ascribe the psalm to him. They then think of the many times he was encircled by danger. But whoever the author, it is certainly a psalm that has brought comfort to believers in fearful times throughout the ages. It can bring comfort to you as well. It is important to understand what the promises mean and also to see that there are conditions for these promises. Today will be an overview.

*1.   What stood out to you from the introduction to this chapter?

Read Psalm 91 in its entirety.
*2.   What are some of the promises that stand out to you upon your overview reading? (Give verse references.)

*3.   What conditions do you find in this psalm for the promises to be fulfilled? (Give verse references.)

*4.   What evidence can you find in the psalm that God is not promising freedom from trouble? (Give verse references.)

Listen to "Under the Shadow" and sing along.

Day Two: Under the Shadow

You can probably think of only a few people in whom you truly confide. Many people may be precious to you, but only a few come into that secret place. It is a mutual decision: they must love and trust you enough to come that close, and you must trust them enough to confide your innermost soul to them.

It is similar with the Lord. He wishes all believers would come into His secret place, but not all choose to fly to the Lord for shelter. They would rather fly to an arm of flesh for comfort. And He does not reveal Himself in the same way to all believers. He does not give the same comfort to all believers.

> *What intimate and unrestrained communion does this describe! . . . This Almighty Friend has admitted his chosen one to his "secret place." It is almost too wonderful to be true. It is almost too presumptuous a thought for such creatures as we are to entertain. But he himself permits it, desires it, teaches us to realise that it is communion to which he calls us. . . . He wishes us to know him, and by his Word and by his Spirit he puts himself before us. Ah! it is not his fault if we do not know him. It is our own carelessness.*[2]
>
> Mary Duncan, Under The Shadow *(1867)*

Listen to "Under the Shadow" (track 7). Learn the first verse.

*5. What is the promise and the condition of Psalm 91:1?

> *Every child of God looks toward the inner sanctuary and the mercy-seat, yet all do not dwell in the most holy place; they run to it at times, and enjoy occasional approaches, but they do not habitually reside in the mysterious presence.*[3]
>
> Charles Spurgeon

6. Meditate on the names of God used in these opening verses and see if you can discern why each would be significant as a place of safety.
    A. Most High

B. Almighty (*Shaddai:* sufficient or all powerful, cf. Genesis 17:1)

C. The Lord (*Jehovah:* self-existent or eternal, cf. Exodus 3:14-15)

D. *my* God (general term made intimate by possessive pronoun)

*7.   There are also four metaphors. Meditate on each, visualize the word picture, and explain its significance to you.
   *A. shelter or hiding place (cf. Psalm 31:20)

   *B. shadow (cf. Song of Songs 2:3)

"Shadow," as in Song of Songs, intimates intimacy. You must be very close to someone to sit in his shadow. It also intimates a shielding from the harsh sun and "the shade of the king" was a widespread metaphor in Near Eastern kingship[4] (cf. Lam. 4:20). When you lived under the shadow of the king, you were under his protection. Oswald Chambers associates it with rest, as one might rest in the shade, or as one might feel secure under a good king's protection. He contrasts it with fretting:

Fretting rises from our determination to have our own way. Our Lord never worried and was never anxious, because His purpose was never to fulfill His own plans, but to fulfill God's plans. . . . Have you been propping up that foolish soul of yours with the idea that your circumstances are too much for God to handle? Set all your opinions and speculations aside and "abide under the shadow of the Almighty."[5]

C. refuge (cf. Psalm 46:1-3)

The idea of refuge in the psalm seems to be that of a secure, protective area guaranteed by Yahweh himself with his presence.[6]

D. fortress (cf. Psalm 71:3)

8.   In your own life, what dangers surround you?

*9.   What do you need to do to draw closer to the Lord, to dwell under the shadow of His wings?

Day Three: He Will Cover You with His Feathers

The word picture in Psalm 91:4 is that of a mother bird spreading out her wings to cover and to shield her babies from harm. Anne Graham Lotz writes,

Our Father is Almighty, but He is not macho. His tender sensitivity to His children reveals a mother's heart.[7]

I am thankful for the maternal attributes of God, just as I am thankful that I was blessed to grow up in a home that had both mother and father. I often feared my father, and that fear helped me to choose the right. But when I was hurting, when I was suffering, it was my mother who brought me comfort. When I faced childhood illnesses, she fluffed my pillows, brought me 7-Up and chicken noodle soup, and rocked me in her loving arms. When a teenage boy broke my heart she didn't tell me that I was silly to care so much about a gangly youth, she held me in her gentle arms and wept with me.

Even though I am middle-aged, I *still* need a mother. There are days when the world is so unfair and my heart is breaking. Does Jesus see? Does Jesus care?

Oh, yes.

In order to come under the shadow of the Lord, in order to rest in His comforting arms, we must be willing to die to ourselves, to controlling our lives, and to sin. Remember how Jesus wept over Jerusalem? He said,

O Jerusalem, Jerusalem, you who kill the prophets and stone those sent to you, how often I have longed to gather your children together, as a hen gathers her chicks under her wings, but you were not willing.
Matthew 23:37

He would have protected Jerusalem from the coming destruction. He would have gathered her children together, as a hen gathers her chicks under her wings. But they were not willing to die to their sin, to their own control.

Are we willing?

Listen to track 7 and sing along with "Under the Shadow."

10.   What maternal attributes of God can you see in the following passages? What comfort do these pictures give you in your life right now?
     A. John 14:18

     B. Revelation 7:17

11.   Meditate on Psalm 91:3.
     A. What is the first calamity from which God can save you? What do you think this means? (cf. Psalm 140:1-5)

     B. The second calamity of verse 3, Psalm 91, "a pestilence," may be a general poetic picture of sin, disease, or trouble. However, it may also refer to being delivered from a thing decreed in heaven, as when God decrees consequences for sin. How is this exemplified in Psalm 78:50 (cf. Exodus 15:26)?

12. Meditate on Psalm 91:4.
    *A. Describe the word picture and the images it brings to your mind.

    B. Compare the above to Psalm 17:8. What is the prayer in that verse?

    *C. In the *King James Version*, it says, "his truth shall be thy shield." Why is it that we cannot expect to be shielded if we are holding onto sin, onto falsehood?

*13. What things do you tend to rely on for security other than the Lord?

Day Four: For He Will Command His Angels

Did you realize that God may command His angels to protect you? He has done that in the past with His children. Here are just a few examples:

- *An angel of God was placed between the Israelites and Pharaoh's charging army. (Exodus 14:19-20)*

- *God sent His angel to rescue three young men from the fiery furnace.* (Daniel 3:28)

- *An angel shut the mouths of the lions, so they could not harm Daniel.* (Daniel 6:22)

- *An angel rescued Peter from prison. (Acts 12:5-11)*

14. Read the account of *one* of the above examples. Describe what the angel did to protect the child or children of God.

*15. Read Psalm 91:9-10.
    *A. Lest we forget the condition that is attached to the blessings of God, the psalmist pauses here, in verse 9, to repeat it. What is the condition?

    *B. What light does Romans 8:35-36 shed on Psalm 91:10?

16. Look carefully to see what you can discover about angels from the following psalms.
    A. Psalm 8:5

    B. Psalm 34:7

    C. Psalm 35:5-6

    D. Psalm 78:49

    *E. Psalm 91:11-12

    F. Psalm 103:20-21

Angels are an exceeding strong and potent people . . .
a very knowing and a wise people . . .
an exceeding active and expeditious people . . .
a people very faithful to God and to man . . .
Who more fit to protect and defend the saints and people of God?[8]
William Bridge (1600-1670)

17.   When you realize God commands angels to destroy or defend, to bring down the woman who opposes God, or to lift up the woman who trusts Him, how does that impact you for your life today?

Listen to "Under the Shadow" and sing along.

Day Five: I Will Be with Him in Trouble

There are many accounts of God delivering His children from trouble on earth. There are also many accounts of God being with His children as He allows them to go through trouble. Both of these truths are present in the closing of Psalm 91. We can also see these truths in the testimonies of believers.

Corrie ten Boom's amazing account of the presence of God during the Holocaust of World War II is contained in her book *The Hiding Place*. The title seems to have a double meaning. Not only was *The Hiding Place* a physical room where the ten Booms hid Jews, but it seems to refer also to the secret place where they themselves found refuge, even in the horror of the concentration camp. Where was it? *Under the shadow of His wings.*

Through a series of miracles, God rescued Corrie ten Boom's life. However, Corrie's sister, Betsie, died. Yet Betsie herself testified to the Lord's presence. Corrie recalled her dying sister's words:

Tell people . . . there is no pit so deep that He is not deeper still. They will listen to us, Corrie, because we have been here.[9]

Corrie went back that night to peer in the window at Betsie. She saw two nurses carrying Betsie's body. She looked like a carving in old yellow ivory. Corrie could see each rib, and the outline of teeth through the parchment cheeks. . . . Corrie flew into the room, overwhelmed with grief. And then the Lord performed a miracle for Corrie. Instead of an emaciated corpse, Corrie saw a miraculous transformation. This is her account of that moment:

Lord Jesus . . . what are you giving me?

For there lay Betsie, her eyes closed as if in sleep, her face full and young. The care lines, the grief lines, the deep hollows of hunger and disease were simply gone. . . . There was the Betsie of heaven, bursting with joy and health. Even her hair was graciously in place as if an angel had ministered to her.[10]

*18. What are the conditions and the promises stated in Psalm 91:14-15?

*19. What similar thought do you find in the following two verses?
I will be with him in trouble (Psalm 91:15b).

When you pass through the waters, I will be with you (Isaiah 43:2a).

It is impossible that any ill should happen to the man who is beloved of the Lord; the most crushing calamities can only shorten his journey and hasten him to his reward. Ill to him is no ill, but only good in a mysterious form. Losses enrich him, sickness is his medicine, reproach is his honour, death is his gain. No evil in the strict sense of the word can happen to him, for everything is overruled for good. Happy is he who is in such a case. He is secure where others are in peril, he lives where others die.[11]
Charles Spurgeon

*20. What do you think you will remember from Psalm 91?

Prayer Time
Pray through Psalm 91:1-2 and Psalm 91:14-15, a verse at a time, followed by conversational prayer. Close by singing "Under the Shadow" together.

Eight

As a Father Has Compassion

Charles Spurgeon has called Psalm 103 "a Bible in itself," and says "it might alone almost suffice for the hymn-book of the church." His love for this psalm is evident in his description:

> As in the lofty Alps some peaks rise above all others, so among even the inspired Psalms there are heights of song which overtop the rest. This one hundred and third Psalm has ever seemed to us to be the Monte Rosa of the divine chain of mountains of praise, glowing with a ruddier light than any of the rest.[1]

This psalm was sung when believers came together for a time of thanksgiving. In Scotland, the one hundred and third Psalm often accompanies communion, for it is a song that rejoices in God's forgiving grace. There is not one sentence of supplication, not one prayer request, in the whole psalm. It teaches us *how* to praise, a lesson we dearly need.

The word picture highlighted in the song "As a Father Has Compassion" is that of a father's concern for his erring child. We are as helpless as babies, as frail as flowers that wilt under the scorching sun. If God were to turn upon us, we would quickly crumble to dust. But God knows this. He made us. Therefore He does not treat us as our sins deserve, but has compassion on us. He lifts us from the pit and renews our strength like an eagle's. Although we, in our frailty, are like the fading flower, God's grace can allow us to have an eternal impact. His tender mercies extend to those who fear Him from generation to generation, and His righteousness extends to their children's children.

Listen to "As a Father Has Compassion" on track 8 of your Integrity CD.

As a Father Has Compassion

As a father has compassion
On his children
So the Lord has compassion
On those who fear Him
For He knows how we are formed
He remembers that we are dust

But from everlasting to everlasting
The Lord's love is with those who fear Him
But from everlasting to everlasting
The Lord's love is with those who fear Him
And His righteousness
With their children's children

Don Harris
© 1993 Integrity's Hosanna! Music /ASCAP
Soloist: Cathy Riso

Warm-Up

It may seem strange that the Lord Almighty would desire creatures to sit around saying nice things to Him. C.S. Lewis said, "I don't want my dog to bark approval of my books."[2] So why is it, do you think, that God commands us to praise Him? Give one reason. (There are many.)

Day 1: Bless the Lord, O My Soul

Psalm 103 is bracketed by the opening and closing:

Bless the LORD, O my soul (KJV)

David, as he often does, talks to his soul. This time he is instructing it to bless the Lord and to do it fervently. To "bless" is more than to praise. It means "to praise with affection and gratitude."[3] It is the difference between Tevye, in *Fiddler on the Roof*, saying to his wife that she should know he loves her because he's been married to her for so long and the Shulammite maiden in the Song of Songs saying,

*Like an apple tree among the trees of the forest
is my lover among the young men.
I delight to sit in his shade,
and his fruit is sweet to my taste.
He has taken me to the banquet hall,
and his banner over me is love.
Strengthen me with raisins,
refresh me with apples,
for I am faint with love.*

Song of Songs 2:3-5

Although blessing the Lord with our words of love is definitely necessary for our own spiritual health, I also believe that God longs to hear it. He is relational. He is our Bridegroom who longs for words of intimacy. What bridegroom wants an apathetic bride? Or a bride who tells him she loves him out of duty rather than passion? Philip Yancey says, "The words of the prophets sound like the words of a lovers' quarrel drifting through thin apartment walls."[4] God has loved us, with such a great love, yet we have lost our devotion for Him. He cries out through Jeremiah:

*I remember the devotion of your youth,
how as a bride you loved me
and followed me through the desert*

Jeremiah 2:2

We have hurt our Bridegroom by our apathy. And we please Him with our genuine and fervent praise.

It is also just and right that we praise Him. If a king passed by and no one even stood to honor him, would that not be wrong? Surely the King of kings deserves our honor. Therefore David lectures his soul to bless the Lord, and after talking to his soul, he then talks to "all his inmost being," that is, his intellect, his emotions, his memory. Drawing upon all his resources, he tells himself to "forget not all his benefits."

God desires praise as well because He knows what happens to us when we forget His goodness to us. This was the lesson of Psalm 78. The Israelites forgot His mighty acts and then turned away from Him, unable to trust Him, unable to pass the knowledge of His goodness to the next generation.

If you know the familiar praise chorus based on the opening verses of Psalm 103, sing it now, to prepare your heart.

*1.   What stood out to you from the introduction to this lesson?

2.   Do you think you are an apathetic or a passionate bride to the Lord? Explain.

3.   Read Psalm 103 as an overview.
     A. What do you see as the central theme?

     B. What word pictures particularly stood out to you?

     *C. What does David instruct his soul to do in the opening and closing phrase?

*4.   Meditate on Psalm 103:1-2.
     *A. To whom is David speaking in the opening?

     My body, God knows, is gross and heavy, and very unfit for so sublime a work. No, my soul, it is thou must do it.[5]
                         Sir Richard Baker (1568-1645)

     B. Now David instructs "all that is within me" to bless the Lord. What does "all that is within me" mean?

*C. Choose one of your capacities (intellect, emotion, or memory) and explain how it could help you to praise the Lord with affection and gratitude.

*D. Now do it. Write your blessing to the Lord here.

*E. What further instruction does David give to his soul in verse 2?

Day 2: Forget Not All His Benefits

C.S. Lewis believed our praise completes our delight.[6] When we have read a wonderful book or eaten at a superb new restaurant—we want to tell others. It completes the delight. A lover who cannot express his love verbally feels frustrated until he does. When he finally says, "I love you," it feels complete.

Praise also helps us to change our focus from ourselves to God. Eugene Peterson defines worship "as that strategy by which we interrupt our preoccupation with ourselves and attend to the presence of God."[7] This is good for us, for when we focus on God, we are less likely to become proud and more apt to keep His commandments. Moses wrote,

> *When you have eaten and are satisfied, praise the LORD your God for the good land he has given you. Be careful that you do not forget the LORD your God, failing to observe his commands, his laws and his decrees that I am giving you this day. Otherwise, when you eat and are satisfied, when you build fine houses and settle down, and when your herds and flocks grow large and your silver and gold increase and all you have is multiplied, then your heart will become proud and you will forget the Lord your God, who brought you out of Egypt, out of the land of slavery. . . . You may say to yourself, "My power and the strength of my hands have produced this wealth for me."*
> *Deuteronomy 8:10-14, 17*

5.   What are some reasons, according to C.S. Lewis and Eugene Peterson, that blessing God is good for us?

*6.   What are some reasons, according to the above passage in Deuteronomy, that we should be careful not to forget God's benefits?

Albert Barnes explains that the word "benefit" refers to all God's dealings, not just what we might typically label "benefits."[8]

*7.   The Lord also desires us to be specific. In Psalm 103:3-5, David gives us categories to help us remember "all His benefits."

A. What is the first benefit according to Psalm 103:3a? Why might this be the most important?

B. From what diseases has the Lord healed you? (Remember not only the diseases of the body, but also the diseases of the soul.)

C. What are some ways the Lord has redeemed your life from "the pit," a word for destruction? (Remember not only salvation, but also ways He has rescued you from the pit of pride, the pit of selfishness, the pit of anger . . .) Think about ways God has compassionately dealt with you as a believer to help you mature, to redeem your life from various forms of destruction.

D. What are some of the good things with which God has satisfied your desires?

E. What are some ways God has renewed your strength? What are some ways He has helped you to fly like an eagle?

An eagle soars on a power other than his own. He finds an updraft of air and soars. Then he finds another updraft and soars. If he were to flap his wings, he would be a very tired eagle![9]

                    Carol Kent

Listen to "As a Father Has Compassion" (track 8) and sing along.

Day 3: As a Father Has Compassion

I am so thankful for this description of the Almighty. If it were not for His tender compassion, where would I be? What would I do? The psalmist sings:

If you, O LORD, kept a record of sins,
O LORD, who could stand?

                    Psalm 130:3

It is in the character of God to forgive those who fear Him and repent:

As far as the east is from the west,
so far has he removed our transgressions from us.

                    Psalm 103:12

Every single day I need His grace—not only for my stubborn and sinful ways, but for my foolishness, and for the immense difficulties of life. And every morning, His mercies are new.

Though he brings grief, he will show compassion,
so great is his unfailing love.
For he does not willingly bring affliction
or grief to the children of men.

                    Lamentations 3:32-33

Because of the LORD's great love we are not consumed,
for his compassions never fail.
They are new every morning;
great is your faithfulness.
                    Lamentations 3:22-23

He is my Father, my Daddy. He hears my cry, tenderly bends down and picks me up, and comforts me in His loving arms.

To prepare your heart for your study, and to bless the Lord, sing (with feeling) "Great Is Thy Faithfulness" (found in most hymnbooks.)

Read Psalm 103:6-14.
8.   What do you learn about God in verse 6?

9.   How does Exodus 2:23-25 illustrate God's compassion for His oppressed children?

*10. For what characteristics of God is the psalmist thankful in Psalm 103:8-10?

*11. What does the word picture of verse 12 mean?

*12. What condition accompanies the assurance given in Psalm 103:11 and appears again in Psalm 103:13?

13.   The fear the psalmist speaks of is a "fear that produces obedience," a fear that springs from a true understanding of a holy God. What light does Hebrews 12:28-29 shed on what constitutes a proper attitude toward God?

Sing "As a Father Has Compassion."

Day 4: He Remembers that We Are Dust

In *Falling in Love with Jesus*, Kathy Troccoli comments that many times God works on her heart by breaking her heart. But she pleads with Him to be gentle, *to kill her softly.*[10] Fortunately, that is the way He is with His children. He does not treat us as our sins deserve. He remembers our fragility. He remembers that we are dust. In the same book, I give an illustration of His recent compassion to me.

> *Because the Lord formed me, He knows, for example, that my gift for intimacy has a dark side. He knows that I tend to cling too tightly to those I love. I had a tremendous struggle letting go of each of my two adult sons, and most recently, Sally, my first daughter to leave the nest. Many mothers tend to worship their children, loving them more than God. I've had to ask myself if that is true of me. I thought I had let Sally go, so then I wondered, "Why does the pain keep increasing? Why do our phone conversations continue to make me so sad? Why does God seem to keep taking her further and further away? Why isn't He making my life turn out the way I expected it to in my relationship with Sally? Is He dealing with me?" Sally and her husband are living in Krakow, Poland, right now and plan to stay over-seas for many years. I've had a lot of heartache and have felt much anxiety about her. My husband said, "You think about her too much. You worry about her too much. You haven't really relinquished her to God, Dee." I remember hearing Corrie ten Boom say that if we cling to someone or something too tightly, our loving Father will pry our fingers away. In fact, I've told thousands of women that this is our weakness as women, we're so relational. We hold our friends, our husbands, and our children too tightly. And so now I wrestle with these questions: "Will I trust God with Sally? Even if, in the future, He allows my beloved child to suffer, will I trust that He is good and that He is God? Will I stop trying to control her life, stop trying to*

shield her from pain? Will I let go, and if she falls, will I believe His arms will catch her?" In my heart I say, "Yes." Yet it is a continual relinquishment. I must constantly lift her up to God and pray, "Help me to trust You. Help me to let go. And Jesus, please kill me softly. Please be gentle with me."[11]

As I look back over the last few years since Sally married I see how many times I was manipulative and unfair—both with Sally and with her young husband. I can actually be thankful now, for the Lord's dealings with me (His *benefits*) for they have helped me grow. I am also thankful that though there have been conse-quences for my sin, He reduced them. He did not treat me as my sins deserved. He did not give me either death or an irreversible breach with my daughter. He remembered that I am but dust. He knows how easily I would crumble under His wrath. He also saw my tears and heard my pleadings for a changed heart and for a heart that could trust Him with Sally. He knows I do fear Him. And as a father has compassion on his children, so the Lord had compassion on me.

Sing "As a Father Has Compassion" (track 8). Can you sing along without looking at the lyrics?

*14. Can you think of an area where you struggled to obey God, and He dealt with you, and finally brought restoration into your life? If so, share briefly (one breath!) to encourage the others in your group and to "praise the Lord in the congregation."

Read Psalm 103:13-16.
15.   What stands out to you upon this reading?

16.   How do the following passages support the truth that "we are dust?"
    A. Genesis 2:7

B. Genesis 3:19

C. Job 34:14-15

17. How is the concept in the above verses repeated in Psalm 103:15-16?

18. Where in your spiritual and physical life do you see frailty?

Spend time in prayer, specifically confessing your spiritual frailties to God. Ask Him to give you a heart of repentance.

Day 5: But from Everlasting to Everlasting

Man, left to himself, is like the flower that passes away. *But*, with God, man can have an impact that lasts, even to his children's children, even to children yet to be born.

As I walk in the fear of the Lord, I know I can have an eternal impact. He has blessed me to see it happen before my very eyes. When "Shout to the Lord" comes on the radio, my six-year-old granddaughter Emily closes her eyes in rapture. Even four-year-old Jessamyn sings along:

My Jesus, my Savior . . .

When I number my years, according to Psalm 90, I realize how fleeting is my life:

The length of our days is seventy years—
or eighty, if we have strength;
yet their span is but trouble and sorrow,
for they quickly pass, and we fly away.
                                    Psalm 90:10

19.   Number your days, according to Psalm 90. What does this teach you?

20.   What do you learn about the Lord in Psalm 103:19?

> *Men should learn not to measure his [God's] power by that of man, since it has under its control all kingdoms and dominions.*[12]
> *John Calvin*

21   What four groups are told to praise the Lord in Psalm 103:20-21?

*22. What contrast do you see between Psalm 103:14-16 and Psalm 103:17-19?

23.   What do you learn about angels? (Also called here heavenly hosts.)

*24. What do you expect to remember about this week's lesson?

Prayer Time

Review your answers to question 6 in this lesson silently. Then pray through Psalm 103:1-5 together, a verse at a time, followed by conversational praise. Imagine the Lord listening, like a bridegroom eager to hear his bride expressing her love. Close by singing "As a Father Has Compassion."

Nine

I Hope in Your Word

*W*hen health fails, when the world disappoints, when loved ones let us down—the Word of God is constant, faithful, and sure. Psalm 119, which exalts the Word of God, is one that has awed and fascinated spiritual giants of old.

St. Augustine delayed writing on Psalm 119 until the rest of his commentary was complete because, he said,

> *It always exceeded the powers of my intent thought and the utmost grasp of my faculties . . . I cannot show how deep it is.*[1]

Matthew Henry preached twenty-two sermons on Psalm 119, one for each of its twenty-two octrains, eight verse poems that follow the twenty-two letters of the Hebrew alphabet. The impetus for this started with his father, Philip Henry. Matthew Henry writes in his biography of his father,

> *He advised us to take a verse of this Psalm every morning to meditate upon, and so go over the Psalm twice in the year; and that, saith he, will bring you to be in love with all the rest of the Scriptures. He often said, "All grace grows as the love to the word of God grows."*[2]

Charles Spurgeon calls this psalm a star among the psalms of the first and greatest magnitude. He devoted 337 pages in his commentary to Psalm 119 alone. He says,

> *The manner it is composed in is very elegant.*
> *The matter it is composed of is very excellent.*[3]

C.S. Lewis describes the language of Psalm 119 as the language of a man "ravished by moral beauty."[4] What is it about the Word of God that overwhelms the psalmist? Is it the delight in its order? Is it the confidence in the power? Is it the awe of its beauty?

One picture will not do, so Psalm 119 overflows with images from a man who has learned to "hope in God's Word." We learn that:

to study them is to find treasure (v. 14)
they are like songs one sings on a long and difficult journey (v. 54)
they are more precious than silver or gold (v. 72)
they are sweeter than honey to his soul (v. 103)
they are a lamp unto his feet, a light unto his path (v. 105)

It is by far the longest psalm. In Scotland, when George Wishart, Bishop of Edinburgh, was facing execution, he availed himself of the custom of the times to have a psalm sung before the condemned dropped from the scaffold. Shrewdly, he chose Psalm 119, and pardon arrived before two-thirds of the psalm had been sung.[5]

How can we possibly hope to study this psalm in a week?

We cannot. But we will look at two octrains and, within those, concentrate on the verses in the song "I Hope in Your Word." When my husband completed his two-year study of the psalms aided by Spurgeon, he suggested I ask Integrity music if they might have a song inspired by the seventh octrain of Psalm 119, for it had ministered to him profoundly. We were both so pleased when they did! And when we heard it, our eyes filled with tears.

Listen to "I Hope in Your Word" (track 9).

I Hope in Your Word

Remember the word to Your servant
Upon which You have caused me to hope
This is my comfort in my affliction
For Your word has given me life
(Repeat)

I rise before the dawning
Of the morning
And cry for help
I hope in Your word
(Repeat)

Harlan Rogers
© 1994 Integrity's Hosanna! Music/ASCAP
Soloist: Melodie Crittenden

Warm-Up

Thy statutes have been my songs in the house of my pilgrimage.
Psalm 119:54 (KJV)

I set your instructions to music and sing them as I walk this pilgrim way.
Psalm 119:54 (TM)

Name one of the songs (or phrases from that song) from our study that has come back to your memory as you journey through this often difficult life.

Day 1: The Comfort of the Word

The seventh octrain of Psalm 119, verses 49-56, deals with the comfort of the Word. It is has similarities to Psalm 1, yet uniquely stresses how placing our hope in the Word can bring comfort when we are suffering.

It opens with the primary reason the Word gives us hope: God's promises are sure. Therefore, when we are afflicted, His promises can sustain us, and quicken (KJV) us, a concept we will explore. Even when we are ridiculed, if we keep our eyes focused on the promises, we can be impervious to that ridicule. We do not cave in to the temptations of the ungodly or to discouragement about our choices, because we realize, with horror, the end of the ungodly. The Scriptures (especially the psalms) become our songs, sustaining us as we travel through this transitory earthly life to our real home in heaven. The octrain concludes by saying that real comfort and joy come from *obeying* the Word.

*1.   What did you learn about Psalm 119 from the introduction?

Read Psalm 119:49-56 carefully.
*2.   Put the main thought of this octrain in your own words. Then back it up with verse references.

Read the seventh octrain (Psalm 119:49-56) in *The Living Bible*:

> *Never forget your promises to me your servant, for they are my only hope. They give me strength in all my troubles; how they refresh and revive me! Proud men hold me in contempt for obedience to God, but I stand unmoved. From my earliest youth I have tried to obey you; your Word has been my comfort. I am very angry with those who spurn your commands. For these laws of yours have been my source of joy and singing through all these years of my earthly pilgrimage. I obey them even at night and keep my thoughts, O Lord, on you. What a blessing this has been to me—to constantly obey.*

3.   Meditate on the above ways the Word of God gives comfort and explain:
  A. How might the Word of God give strength in trouble?

  B. How might the Word of God keep you from caving in when proud people mock your obedience?

  C. How might the Word of God be a source of joy and singing?

  D. How might obedience to the Word of God be a blessing?

Day 2: Remember the Word to Your Servant

It is a tender plea. As a child might say to his mother, "Remember you promised that if I put away my toys and took my nap you would take me to the park." He doesn't want to be forgotten, for he has been thinking about the park promise, and it has sustained him as he has obeyed.

In the same way, the mighty promises of God sustain us, and we want Him to remember His promises to us. We have been thinking about promises such as:

> You hear, O LORD, the desire of the afflicted;
> you encourage them, and you listen to their cry,
> defending the fatherless and the oppressed,
> in order that man, who is of the earth, may terrify no more.
> Psalm 10:17-18

> To the faithful you show yourself faithful.
> Psalm 18:25a

> The angel of the LORD encamps around those who fear him,
> and he delivers them.
> Psalm 34:7

It isn't as though the Lord *would* forget, for His memory is much better than ours. Isaiah reminds us,

> Can a mother forget the baby at her breast
> and have no compassion on the child she has borne?
> Though she may forget,
> I will not forget you!
> Isaiah 49:15

Yet this is how the psalmist phrases the request, for, as Charles Spurgeon says, it is "after the manner of men when they plead with one another."[6]

After the psalmist asks *the Lord* to remember what He has said, he then uses the word *remember* twice in reference to himself. They (God and the psalmist) each have a kind of remembering to do that issues an action, not just mental awareness.

I remember your ancient laws, O LORD, and I find comfort in them.
Psalm 119:52

I remember your name, O LORD, and I will keep your law.
Psalm 119:55

Sing along with "I Hope in Your Word" (track 9).

Read Psalm 119:49-56 again.
*4.   What does the psalmist ask of God in verse 49? Why?

God's promises are his bonds. Sue him on his bond. He loves that we should wrestle with him by his promises.[7]
Richard Sibbes (1577-1635)

Understanding the above concept can transform your prayer life with the mighty power of the Word. For example, I often wake in the night, and after a time of prayer, I ask the Lord to give me sleep. I wrestle with Him on the promise He gives in Psalm 127:2:

He grants sleep to those He loves.

So I pray,

Precious Lord, You tell me I am Your beloved. Please grant me sleep, as You promise You will.

Then His Spirit will remind me that there is a condition that accompanies that promise, for the context of this promise is Psalm 127:1:

Unless the LORD builds the house, its builders labor in vain.
Unless the LORD watches over the city, the watchmen stand guard in vain.

So then I pray,

Yes, Lord, I have been carrying these worries about my family and life—I cast them on You. I trust You to watch over my family and my life. I cast these burdens on You. I fall back into Your safe arms. As I do that, please grant me sleep.

As I obey and trust, then He gives me His promised gift of sleep. This is prayer with power. We can ask Him to remember His Word to His servant. He may remind us of conditions, but we have opened up a dialogue with Him.

5.   How is the petitioner's tender request of the Lord to remember used in the following instances?
    A. 1 Samuel 1:11

    B. Psalm 132:1

    C. Luke 23:42

6.   When the psalmist says, "Remember the word to your servant," what do you think he is feeling and desiring?

*7.   Explain how the psalmist use the word "remember" in regard to himself. In each of these cases, explain what he has remembered and also the action that proceeded as a result of his remembering.
    A. Psalm 119:52

When we see no present display of the divine power it is wise to fall back upon the records of former ages, since they are just as available as if the transactions were yesterday, seeing the Lord is always the same. . . .

Moreover, if we are advanced in years we have the providences of our early days to review.[8]

Charles Spurgeon

B. Psalm 119:55

It is but mockery of God, to desire him to remember his promise made to us, when we make no conscience of the promise we have made to him.[9]

William Cowper (1566-1619)

*8.   What promise do you want the Lord to remember that He has made to you in His Word? Is there a condition attached to the promise? If so, what is it?

Day 3: This Is My Comfort in My Affliction

The woman of the world may cling to her beauty or to her youth or to her wealth and say, "This is my comfort." The woman who has given herself over to the lust of the flesh may cling to sexual pleasure or to food or to alcohol and say, "This is my comfort." But we want to be women who believe with our whole hearts that God's life-giving promises are true and who testify, "This word of hope is my comfort." We want to sincerely sing,

This is my comfort in my affliction,
for Your word has given me life.

Psalm 119:50 (NKJV)

The last phrase is full of meaning and various translators have sought to catch it:

your promises rejuvenate me

Psalm 119:50b (TM)

Thy word has revived me

Psalm 119:50b (NASB)

for thy word hath quickened me
Psalm 119:50b (KJV)

It contains the idea of bringing life to the dead through the power of the Word. For a long time, my husband has prayed daily that the Lord would *quicken* me in my ministry. He wants me to know the life-giving power of God, through His Word, in what He has called me to do. I am so thankful for this prayer. I do not want to stand before crowds of women without His quickening. Neither do I want the heavy responsibility of writing without His quickening. In the challenging role of mother, mother-in-law, and grandmother, I need His quickening. But whatever role God has called you to, be it mother or mentor, soul winner or surgeon, writer or waitress . . . you need His quickening. It makes the difference between being a dead man walking or a vibrant child of God; between moving aimlessly, as Susannah Wesley warned against, "like straws upon the river," or having purpose, direction, and meaning; and between being without hope, without peace, and without comfort in affliction, or having all of these sweet consolations to sustain you.

Sing along with "I Hope in Your Word."

*9.   Quite honestly, what would you say is your comfort? How well does it do the job? Explain.

10.   What brings comfort to the psalmist in his affliction? What are some ways that this would happen?

Meditate on Psalm 119:51-53.
11.   The psalmist is ridiculed by unbelievers. But he is able to stand firm. Why, according to the following?
    A. Psalm 119:51-52

B. Psalm 119:53

The *King James Version* translates verse 53, "Horror hath taken hold upon me because of the wicked that forsake thy law." In perhaps the most famous sermon of all time, "Sinners in the Hand of an Angry God," Jonathan Edwards proclaimed,

> *Who knows the power of God's anger? How dreadful is the state of those that are daily and hourly in danger of this great wrath and infinite misery! But this is the dismal case of every soul in this congregation that has not been born again, however moral and strict, sober and religious, they may otherwise be. Oh that you would consider it, whether you be young or old!*
>
> *If we knew that there was one person, and but one, in the whole congregation, that was to be the subject of this misery, what an awful thing would it be to think of! . . . But, alas! Instead of one, how many is it likely will remember this discourse in hell!*[10]

Read Psalm 119:54-56.
In this seventh octrain, as in Psalm 78, memory is stressed. We are *not to forget* what God has done for us. How can we remember the mighty acts of God? How can we remember the promises of the Word? The psalmist has developed some habits that help him.

*12. From Psalm 119:54, describe a habit that helped the psalmist remember the Word.

> *Travellers sing to deceive the tediousness of the way; so did David. . . . Great is the comfort that cometh in by singing of Psalms with grace in our hearts.*[11]
> *John Trapp*

13. Are you singing the psalms you have learned in this study? Are you listening to them at other times than to prepare your lesson? If so, share and comment.

14.   From Psalm 119:55, describe another habit that helped the psalmist remember the Word.

He was so earnest after the living God that he woke up at dead of night to think upon him. These were David's Night Thoughts.[12]
Charles Spurgeon

*15.   From Psalm 119:56b, describe a habit that increased the psalmist's memory and his understanding of the Word.

The Rabbins have an analogous saying: The reward of a precept is a precept. He who keeps one precept, to him God grants, as if by way of reward, the ability to keep another and more difficult precept.[13]
Simon de Muis (1587-1644)

16.   Can you share an example of how the above has been true for you, how obedience to a truth from God's Word has been a blessing and has given you the strength and desire to obey in other areas?

Day 4: I Cry with All My Heart

Are you beginning to long for a more intimate relationship with the Savior? Is it your heart's cry to fall more deeply in love with Jesus? Philip Yancey says,

More than any book in the Bible, Psalms reveals what a heartfelt, soul-starved, single-minded relationship with God looks like.[14]

The nineteenth octrain of Psalm 119 (vv. 145-152) is a cry of the heart, childlike in its earnestness, poignant in its persistence. The psalmist cries before the dawning of the morning, he cries through the day, he cries through the night watches. When God does not immediately respond, the psalmist returns to prayer, pleading with God to *quicken* him, or to give him new strength as he waits. Not only does he pray, with tears, he meditates on the Word of God. He wants intimacy. He is in dire need and wants help, the preservation of his life, and an answer from God, who is the Love of his life. From the time he was a boy, he has put his hope in God and His Word. His love and passion for the Lord has only grown with maturity, though the sweet earnestness of a child remains. Now, as in the seventh octrain, he reminds God,

> *I rise before the dawning of the morning,*
> *and cry for help; I hope in Your word*
> $\qquad$ *Psalm 119:147* (NKJV)

Sing along with "Streams of Water" (track 2) and "I Hope in Your Word" (track 9).

Meditate on Psalm 119:145-152.
*17. Find phrases in this octrain that evidence a "heartfelt, soul-starved" desire for God.

18.   When is the last time you were in such need or had such a strong desire that you "cried to God with your whole heart"?

> *Heart-cries are the essence of prayer. . . . It is to be feared that many never cried to God with their whole heart in all of their lives. . . . True supplicants are not satisfied with the exercise itself, they have an end and object in praying, and they look out for it.*[15]
> $\qquad$ *Charles Spurgeon*

19.   When was the last time that God answered a cry from your whole heart?

*20. Based on this octrain, how do you think the psalmist mixed prayer with his meditation on the Word? What could you learn from this for your own devotional life?

21. How many times, in this octrain alone, did he mention calling for help from the Lord?

Personal Prayer Exercise

Is there a Scripture or a promise from Scripture that you can cling to and wrestle with God over concerning your present affliction? Find it, and then pray. Read the following examples, and then make this prayer exercise your own.

Example # 1: Ellen

Father, You have said that it is not good for man to be alone (Genesis 2:18). Lord, I do not feel called to be single. I so desire a godly husband. Father, I am delighting in You (Psalm 37:4), and I claim Your promise that You will give me the desire of my heart. Please give me that desire, or change that desire so that I might be contented as a single woman.

Then Ellen would sing:

*Remember the word to Your servant
Upon which You have caused me to hope*

Then Ellen would praise:

*This is my comfort in my affliction
For Your word has given me life*

Then Ellen would petition boldly again, asking God to help her and to honor His promises:

Please give me the desire of my heart, or change that desire so that I might be contented as a single woman.

Finally, she would sing:

I rise before the dawning of the morning
And cry for help
I hope in Your Word

Example # 2: Sandy

Father, you have promised that if I seek You and Your righteousness, that You
will meet my needs (Matthew 6:33). I am struggling to pay my rent and buy
groceries. I ask that you would meet my needs, on the basis of Your Word.

Then Sandy would sing:

Remember the word to Your servant
Upon which You have caused me to hope

Then Sandy would praise:

This is my comfort in my affliction
For Your word has given me life

Then Sandy would petition boldly again, asking God to help her and to honor His promises:

Please meet my needs as I seek You and Your Kingdom first.

Finally, she would sing:

I rise before the dawning of the morning
And cry for help
I hope in Your Word

Now it is your turn.

Day 5: I Rise Before the Dawning of the Morning

In this octrain, as in Psalm 1, the psalmist meditates on the Word of God day and night. Here the psalmist sings, "I rise before the dawning of the morning . . ."

There are many sound physical and spiritual arguments for cultivating the discipline of rising early and meeting with the Lord. If your body does not naturally have a "morning clock," cultivating it could greatly increase the fruitfulness of your life. If you discipline yourself to get up with the alarm, soon you will find that you have no trouble going to sleep at a sensible hour. In time, it will be your natural rhythm. In biblical days, people slept from sunset to sunrise, and there is much support for following this pattern. Sleep specialists recommend sleeping when it is dark, rather than light, and going to bed at approximately the same time each evening and waking at about the same time each morning.

Spiritual reasons for rising early have to do with productivity and preparedness. Most people tend to be more productive in the morning than at night. (Today many spend those evening hours in front of television.) Matthew Henry wrote,

> David was an early riser, which perhaps contributed to his eminency. . . . the first thing he did in the morning, before he admitted any business, was to pray; when his mind was most fresh and in the best frame. If our first thoughts in the morning be of God, it will help to keep us in his fear all day long.[16]

I love the precious morning hours. It is so quiet and beautiful, and the phone seldom rings between five and eight in the morning. As soon as I have my shower and make my coffee, I am ready to meet with my Bridegroom. I am eager for His sweet morning kisses and I am in need of His instructions for the day.

> He who rushes from his bed to his business and waiteth not to worship, is as foolish as though he had . . . dashed into battle without arms or armour. Be it ours to bathe in the softly flowing river of communion with God, before the heat of the wilderness and the burden of the way begin to oppress us.[17]
> Charles Spurgeon

Having said all that, I know it is possible to be legalistic about the above. There may be seasons in your life, such as when you are nursing an infant or working a night shift, when it would not be wise to set an alarm and wake early. But the fervor the psalmist has for God's Word is a fervor for which we should pray, so that we are continually looking to it, morning, noon, and evening.

Sing "I Hope in Your Word" (track 9).

22. In the following verses, explain when the psalmist is crying to God and meditating on His Word:
    A. Psalm 119:147

    B. Psalm 119:148

23. On the basis of the above Scriptures and the introductory comments to this day, is there an application you feel you should make to your life? If so, what is it?

24. Which verse in Psalm 1 best summarizes Psalm 119:145-152?

25. Notice the play on the concept of location in Psalm 119:150-151. Who is near and from what are they far? Who else is near?

*26. What do you think you will remember from this week's lesson?

Sing along with "I Hope in Your Word" (track 9).

Prayer Time

If you are willing and find it prudent, share the earnest desire of your heart, the one you shared in your personal prayer exercise on day 4. Lift it up and let the others support you. When there is a silence, another woman can lift up her earnest desire.

Close by singing "I Hope in Your Word."

Ten

I Was Made to Praise You

Hopefully you have come to realize through this journey that you are loved by God, that His thoughts are toward you, and that He desires for you to stay close to Him. As we review verses you have memorized through the help of the praise songs, you will be reminded:

He wants you to delight in His Word.
He sees your tears and hears your prayers.
He wants you to put your hope in Him all through the day.
He is willing to wash you and make you whiter than snow.
He longs for you to stay under the shadow of His wings.
He has compassion for you, as a father has compassion on his children.
He made you, and He remembers that you are dust.
He desires His Word to be your comfort in your affliction.

We will close this week with a review, and I think you will be surprised to see how many verses you have learned. I pray you will keep them always in your heart, pray through them, cling to them, and use them to praise your Lord.

For indeed, you were made to praise Him. In choosing a psalm with which to close this study, I was drawn to Psalm 139 and to the song inspired by it, "I Was Made to Praise You."

Listen to "I Was Made to Praise You" (track 10).

I Was Made to Praise You

I was made to praise You
I was made to glorify Your name
In every circumstance
To find a chance to thank You
I was made to love You
I was made to worship at Your feet
And to obey You, Lord
I was made for You
(repeat)

I will always praise You
I will always glorify Your name
In every circumstance
I'll find a chance to thank You
I will always love You
I will always worship at Your feet
And I'll obey You, Lord
I was made for You
I was made for You

Chris Christensen
© 1988 Integrity's Hosanna! Music/ASCAP
Soloist: Karen Childers

Warm-Up
Consider your body and describe a part that is "fearfully and wonderfully made."
What amazes you? What does this teach you about your Creator?

Day 1: You Are Familiar with All My Ways
I know I have a deceitful heart (Jeremiah 17:9) and that I often do not even see
my sinful motives. I may convince myself that I am doing something to bring
praise to God when I am really seeking to bring praise to me.

I know I have a complex body, a body that is fearfully and wonderfully made, but
it is often difficult to understand. Am I blue because I have neglected proper

sleep or nutrition? Could it be hormonal? Am I getting sick?

I know I have been given limitations to teach me to depend on the Lord, and I have been given talents to help me serve Him—but do I always assess each with sober judgment, as I am told to do? (Romans 12:3)

How can we possibly know our hearts, our talents, our complex bodies, and our very souls? Only through the Spirit of God, who knit us together in our mother's womb, can we hope to have any true understanding of ourselves. He knows us so well, being familiar with *all* our ways, that it is only in submission to Him and through His revelation that we can have any hope of knowing ourselves.

O Lord, You are the God of the early mornings, the God of the late nights, the God of the mountain peaks, and the God of the sea. But, my God, my soul has horizons further away than those of early mornings, deeper darkness than the nights of earth, higher peaks than any mountain peaks, greater depths than any sea in nature. You who are the God of all these, be my God. I cannot reach to the heights or to the depths; there are motives I cannot discover, dreams I cannot realize. My God, search me.[1]
Oswald Chambers

*1.　What stood out to you from the introduction to this chapter?

Read Psalm 139 in its entirety.
*2.　What stands out to you in this overview reading?

3.　What are some of the ways you see the omniscience of the Lord in the opening six verses? (Give verse references.)

4.　What are some of the ways you see the omnipresence of the Lord in the next six verses? (Give verse references.)

The brightness of this Psalm is like unto a sapphire stone, or Ezekiel's "terrible crystal"; it flames out with such flashes of light as to turn night into day. . . . this holy song casts a clear light to the uttermost parts of the sea, and warns us against that practical atheism which ignores the presence of God, and so makes shipwreck of the soul.[2]
Charles Spurgeon

5.   Why is God's omniscience and omnipresence both wonderful and terrible?

6.   How will reflecting upon this impact you today?

Day Two: You Knit Me Together in My Mother's Womb

Each time I was pregnant, I daily thought about the little one growing in my womb and wondered at the skill of the One who could knit him or her together so magnificently—in the dark! I found comfort in knowing that His eyes saw their unformed members and that His hands (as those who have done any knitting know) touched every fiber of their being. He planned not only their genetic structure, their hair color, their talents . . . but their days—every one of them. Such knowledge is too wonderful for me.

And why were we made? We are called to glorify God with our lives and to delight in Him. Indeed, we were made to praise Him.

Sing along with "I Was Made to Praise You."

Meditate on Psalm 139:11-18.
*7.   God's ability to see in the dark results in what truth, according to the following?
    *A. Psalm 139:11-12

    B. Job 34:22

*8.   Do you ever delude yourself that you can hide from God, that there are thoughts or actions He cannot see? Explain why this lie hurts you.

In *Falling in Love with Jesus* Kathy Troccoli, who is a single woman, reflects,

> *Do I want to go out and make love? Absolutely. I'm a passionate forty-two-year-old woman. But I don't want what comes with it. Nothing in my life is worth the cost of sacrificing the peace of God. The partying, the sizzle, the chemistry—it's all so attractive in the world—but none of it is worth it. Is it fun? It can be. Does is give pleasure? Absolutely. But I don't know anyone, including myself, who doesn't awaken to emptiness, to the sad realization that the peace of God has slipped away. In the moment, it makes you feel alive. But it's that false aliveness, that false sense of passion, that false sense of euphoria. But Satan encourages us not to stop and think. He says, "Come on, it's great, don't miss it."*
>
> *We finally give in and say, "Okay . . . " And then, **Boom!** He runs off and you're left with this pile of shame and guilt. You get close to the fire and then enter the fire, and find yourself trying to do the Flintstones back peddle. I say it because I've lived it. I've crossed some lines. I've played with fire. . . . I realize now it's all such death and that it breeds death. I want the peace of God more than anything. Sometimes in the peace of God you can feel a little lonely, and that's okay.*[3]

9.   God's ability to see in the dark results in what truth, according to the following?
    A. Psalm 139:15-16

> *He [David] likens the womb of the mother to "the lowest caverns or recesses of the earth." Should an artisan intend commencing a work in some dark cave where there was no light to assist him, how would he set his hand to it? In what way would he proceed? and what workmanship would it prove? The verb "rakam," which means "weave together," is employed to amplify and*

enhance what the Psalmist has just said. David no doubt means figuratively to express the inconceivable skill which appears in the formation of the human body. When we examine it, even to the nails on our fingers, there is nothing which could be altered, without felt inconveniency. . . . Where is the embroiderer who—with all his industry and ingenuity—could execute the hundredth part of this complicated and diversified structure? We need not wonder if God, who formed man so perfectly in the womb, should have an exact knowledge of him after he is ushered into the world.[4]
John Calvin

B. Isaiah 29:15-16

10.   If you have had the privilege of becoming a mother, describe the wonder you felt when you first saw your baby.

11.   Do you ever delude yourself that God made a mistake in the way He created you? Explain why this lie hurts you.

*12.   The fact that God understands your deceitful heart, that He knows how and why He formed you as He did, should lead to what response, according to the following?
    *A. Psalm 139:23-24

B. Psalm 119:73-74

Personal Action Assignment
Be still before the Lord, and allow His Holy Spirit to search you. Remember how He loves you and desires your best. Ask Him what grieves Him in your life. Ask

Him what pleases Him in your life. Write down what His Spirit shows you.

Close this time by singing "Whiter Than Snow."

Day Three: How Precious to Me Are Your Thoughts

The last few years of my life have been a time of tremendous growth, even though I am fifty-five years of age. God has shown me, through the Scripture, through my friendship with Kathy Troccoli, and through some wonderful books by John Eldredge (*The Sacred Romance* and *The Journey of Desire*) just how much God loves me (and you) and desires intimacy with me (and you). It amazes me—for God is so holy, so amazing, why would He desire me? Yet though He needs nothing, He does desire an intimate relationship with me. A.W. Tozer asserted, "God waits to be wanted."[5]

This is something that David seems to have grasped and that made him "a man after God's heart." He knew God desired his love, and he could not stop praising Him for the preciousness of God's thoughts toward him.

> *How precious also are thy thoughts unto me, O God! how great is the sum of them!*
> *If I should count them, they are more in number than the sand: when I awake, I am still with thee.*
> Psalm 139:17-18 (KJV)

This is a truth Charles Spurgeon turned over and over in his mind, and one that gave him great joy. He writes,

> *It should fill us with adoring wonder and reverent surprise that the infinite mind of God should turn so many thoughts towards us who are so insignificant and so unworthy! What a contrast is all this to the notion of those who deny the existence of a personal, conscious God!*[6]

13.   How do you see both God's love to David and David's love to God in Psalm 139:17-18?

Behold David's love to God; sleeping and waking his mind runs upon him. . . . If thou thinkest not often of God, thou lovest him not.[7]
            Francis Taylor, in "God's Glory in Man's Happiness" (1654)

14.   What do you think you will remember about Psalm 139?

In Psalm 139:17, David says, "When I awake, I am still with you." Review the following passage, which you memorized with the help of "I Hope in Your Word." See if you can say it by heart.

I rise before the dawning of the morning,
And cry for help; I hope in Your word.
            Psalm 119:147 (NKJV)

*15.   What do you remember from lesson 9 (particularly days 4 and 5) about the above passage?

Review the following passage, which you memorized with the help of the same song, "I Hope in Your Word." Can you say it by heart?

Remember the word to Your servant,
Upon which You have caused me to hope.
This is my comfort in my affliction,
For Your word has given me life.
            Psalm 119:49-50 (NKJV)

*16.   What do you remember from lesson 9 (particularly days 1-3) about the above passage?

Sing "I Hope in Your Word" in your quiet time.

Review the following passage, which you memorized with the help of "Streams of Water" (track 2). Can you say it by heart?

> *Blessed is the man*
> *who does not walk in the counsel of the wicked*
> *or stand in the way of sinners*
> *or sit in the seat of mockers.*
> *But his delight is in the law of the LORD,*
> *and on his law he meditates day and night.*
> *He is like a tree planted by streams of water.*
> *Psalm 1:1-3a*

*17.   What do you remember from lesson 2 about the above passage?

Close today's quiet time by singing "Streams of Water."

Day Four: The Lord Is Close to the Brokenhearted

Do you carry a wound in your heart? Do you think about a circumstance in your life that you know God had the power to prevent, but He didn't? Do you question, therefore, His love for you? I believe we all have times like that, but then we must return to the unfathomable ways of God. We cannot see the whole picture, nor can we understand His ways. But we can see evidence of His love in the tender way He knit us together in our mother's womb (Psalm 139), in His mighty works on our behalf (Psalm 78), and in His nearness to us when we are brokenhearted, when we are contrite of Spirit (Psalms 10, 34, 51).

To prepare your heart, sing the following three songs:
"The Desire of the Afflicted" (track 3)
"Whiter Than Snow" (track 5)
"As a Father Has Compassion" (track 8)

Review the following verse, which you memorized with the help of "The Desire of the Afflicted." Can you say it by heart?

> *You hear, O LORD, the desire of the afflicted;*
> *you encourage them, and you listen to their cry.*
> Psalm 10:17

*18. What do you remember from lesson 3 (day 1) about the above passage?

Review the following passage, also in "The Desire of the Afflicted." Can you say it by heart?

> *The LORD is close to the brokenhearted*
> *and saves those who are crushed in spirit.*
> *A righteous man may have many troubles,*
> *but the LORD delivers him from them all.*
> Psalm 34:18-19

*19. What do you remember from lesson 3 (days 2-5) about the above?

Review the following passage, which you memorized with the help of "Whiter Than Snow." Can you say it by heart?

> *For I acknowledge my transgressions,*
> *And my sin is ever before me.*
> *Against You, You only, have I sinned,*
> *And done this evil in Your sight—*
> *That You may be found just when You speak,*
> *And blameless when You judge. . . .*
> *Purge me with hyssop, and I shall be clean;*
> *Wash me, and I shall be whiter than snow.*
> Psalm 51:3–4 and 7 (NKJV)

*20. What particularly stood out to you about the above passage from lesson 5 (days 1-4)?

Review the following passage, which you memorized with the help of "As a Father Has Compassion." Can you say it by heart?

As a father has compassion on his children,
so the LORD has compassion on those who fear him;
for he knows how we are formed,
he remembers that we are dust. . . .
But from everlasting to everlasting
the LORD's love is with those who fear him,
And his righteousness with their children's children.
                    Psalm 103:13 and 17

*21. What do you think you will remember about the above passage from lesson 8 (days 1 and 3-5)?

Day Five: I Was Made to Praise You

In "I Was Made to Praise You," we are told:

I was made to praise You
I was made to glorify Your name
In every circumstance
To find a chance to thank You

In studying the psalms, we have studied the heart of David. Surely it can be said of him, that in every circumstance, He poured out His heart to God. If God did not at first respond, David poured out his heart again. He lectured his soul, he reminded himself of the promises of God, and then he waited upon God, until the Spirit "quickened" him, reviving him to praise. We live in a day of passionless believers, how we need to learn from David and ask God to restore our passion, our intimacy, and therefore, our praise for Him.

Prepare your heart by singing "Shout to the Lord," "Give Thanks," and "I Was Made to Praise Him."

Review the following passage, which you memorized with the help of "Why Are You Downcast"(track 5). Can you say it by heart?

Why are you downcast, O my soul?
Why so disturbed within me?
Put your hope in God,
for I will yet praise him,
my Savior and my God.
                              Psalm 42:5

*22. What do you think you will remember concerning your study of the above verse from lesson 4?

Review the following passage, which you studied with the help of "Under the Shadow" (track 7). The lyrics did not follow exactly, though very closely:

He who dwells in the shelter of the Most High
will rest in the shadow of the Almighty.
I will say of the LORD, "He is my refuge and my fortress,
my God, in whom I trust."
                              Psalm 91:1-2

*23. What do you think you will remember concerning your study of the above passage from lesson 7 (days 1 and 2)?

*24. What is your favorite passage from this whole study? Why?

Prayer Time

Pray through the verses you have memorized, as reviewed in this lesson. Close by singing "I Was Made to Praise You."

Sources

Introduction

1. Dee Brestin and Kathy Troccoli, *Falling in Love with Jesus* (Nashville: Word, 2000), n.p.
2. Charles Spurgeon, *The Full Harvest*, vol. 2 of *C.H. Spurgeon Autobiography* (Carlisle, PA: The Banner of Truth Trust, 1995), 147.
3. Dallas Willard, *The Divine Conspiracy: Rediscovering Our Hidden Life in God* (New York: Harper Collins, 1998), 65.

One: Shout to the Lord

1. Philip Yancey, *The Bible Jesus Read* (Grand Rapids: Zondervan, 1999), 109.
2. Yancey, *The Bible Jesus Read*, 112.
3. Charles Spurgeon, *The Treasury of David*, vol. 1, part 1 (Peabody, MA: Hendrickson, n.d.), 324.
4. T.W. Hunt, *The Mind of Christ: The Transforming Power of Thinking His Thoughts* (Nashville: Broadman & Holman, 1995), 114-115.
5. Peter C. Craigie, *Psalms 1-50*, Word Biblical Commentary, ed. David A. Hubbard et al., vol. 19 (Waco, TX: Word, 1983), 203.
6. Rebecca Manley Pippert, *A Heart Like His: The Shaping of Character in the Choices of Life* (Wheaton: Crossway, 1996), 39-40.
7. John Brown, as quoted in Spurgeon, *The Treasury of David*, vol. 1, part 1, 253.
8. John Eldredge, *The Journey of Desire* (Nashville: Thomas Nelson, 2000), 60.
9. Charles Spurgeon, *The Treasury of David*, vol. 1, part 1, 239.
10. George Horne, as quoted in Spurgeon, *The Treasury of David*, vol. 1, part 1, 240.
11. Augustus F. Tholuck, as quoted in Spurgeon, *The Treasury of David*, vol. 1, part 1, 255.
12. Craigie, *Psalms 1-50*, 176.

Two: Planted by Streams of Water

1. J. Vernon McGee, *Psalms: Genesis Section, Psalms 1-41* (Nashville: Thomas Nelson, 1991), 13.
2. Willard, *The Divine Conspiracy: Rediscovering Our Hidden Life in God*, 1-2.
3. Wendy Shalit, *A Return to Modesty: Discovering the Lost Virtue* (New York: Touchstone, 1999), 9-10.
4. Charles Spurgeon, *The Treasury of David*, vol. 3, part 2 (Peabody, MA: Hendrickson, n.d.), 99.
5. Dr. Moffat, as quoted in C.S. Lewis, *Reflections on the Psalms* (New York: Harcourt, Brace and Word, 1958), 56.
6. Charles Spurgeon, *The Treasury of David*, vol. 2, part 1. (Peabody, MA: Hendrickson, n.d.), 67.
7. Corrie ten Boom, *Her Story: The Hiding Place, Tramp for the Lord, Jesus Is Victor* (New York: Inspirational Press, 1995), 151.
8. Charles Spurgeon, *Spurgeon's Expository Encyclopedia: Sermons by Charles H. Spurgeon*, vol. 7 (Grand Rapids: Baker, 1998), 294-99.

Three: The Lord Is Close to the Brokenhearted

1. Craigie, *Psalms 1-50*, 126.
2. Spurgeon, *The Treasury of David*, vol. 1, part 1, 101.
3. Thomas Watson, as quoted in Spurgeon, *The Treasury of David*, vol. 1, part 1, 127.
4. McGee, *Psalms: Genesis Section, Psalms 1-41*, 187.

5. Spurgeon, *The Treasury of David*, vol. 1, part 2, 123.
6. William Gurnall, as quoted in Spurgeon, *The Treasury of David*, vol. 1, part 2, 129.
7. John Calvin, *Calvin's Commentaries*, vol. 4 (Grand Rapids: Baker, 1998), 562.
8. Craigie, *Psalms 1-50*, 280.
9. Spurgeon, *The Treasury of David*, vol. 1, part 2, 126.
10. Dietrich Bonhoeffer, *Psalms: The Prayer Book of the Bible* (Minneapolis: Augsburg Fortress, 1970), 24.
11. Willard, *The Divine Conspiracy: Rediscovering Our Hidden Life in God*, 32.

Four: Why Are You Downcast, O My Soul?
1. Spurgeon, *The Treasury of David*, vol. 1, part 2, 270.
2. Bonhoeffer, *Psalms: The Prayer Book of the Bible*, 9-12.
3. Ibid., 18-19.
4. Lewis, *Reflections on the Psalms*, 51.
5. William Gurnall, as quoted in Spurgeon, *The Treasury of David*, vol. 1, part 2, 283.
6. Dr. Steve Brestin, interview, 3 July 2000.
7. Charles Bradley, as quoted in Spurgeon, *The Treasury of David*, vol. 3, part 2, 142.
8. Spurgeon, *The Treasury of David*, vol. 1, part 2, 273.
9. Ibid., 272.
10. Lyndsey O'Connor, address to Heritage Keepers. Wichita. 15 April 2000.

Five: Whiter than Snow
1. Calvin, *Calvin's Commentaries*, vol. 5, 285.
2. Dietrich Bonhoeffer, *Temptation* (New York: Macmillan, 1953), 116-17.
3. Charles Swindoll, *David: A Man of Passion & Destiny* (Dallas: Word, 1997), 207.
4. Joseph S. Excell, "The Second Book of Samuel," *The Pulpit Commentary*, vol. 4, eds. H.D.M. Spence and Joseph S. Excell (Peabody, MA: Hendrickson, n.d.), 289.
5. Dorian Coover-Cox, interview, 3 August 2000.
6. Beth Moore, *A Heart Like His* (Nashville: Broadman and Holman, 1999), 190.
7. Oswald Chambers, *My Utmost for His Highest* (Grand Rapids: Discovery House, 1992), Nov. 19.
8. Spurgeon, *The Treasury of David*, vol. 1, part 2, 402.
9. Moore, *A Heart Like His*, 195.

Six: Give Thanks
1. Spurgeon, *The Treasury of David*, vol. 2, part 1, 366.
2. Derek Kidner, *Psalms 73-150: A Commentary on Books III-V of the Psalms* (Downers Grove, IL:, InterVarsity Press, 1973), 407.
3 Ibid., 410.
4. Leslie C. Allen, *Psalms 101-150, Word Biblical Commentary*, vol. 21, ed. David A Hubbard et al. (Waco, TX: Word, 1983), 115.

Seven: Under the Shadow of Your Wings
1. Spurgeon, *The Treasury of David*, vol. 2, part 2, 92.
2. Mary Duncan, as quoted in Spurgeon, *The Treasury of David*, vol. 2, part 2, 95.
3. Spurgeon, *The Treasury of David*, vol. 2, part 2, 88.
4. Allen, *Psalms 101-150*, 453.
5. Chambers, *My Utmost for His Highest*, July 4.

6.   Allen, *Psalms 51-100*, 453.
7.   Anne Graham Lotz, *Daily Light Journal* (Nashville: Thomas Nelson, 1999), July 4.
8.   William Bridge, as quoted in Spurgeon, *The Treasury of David*, vol. 2, part 2, 105.
9.   ten Boom, *Her Story: The Hiding Place, Tramp for the Lord, Jesus Is Victor,* 159.
10.   Ibid., 160.
11.   Spurgeon, *The Treasury of David*, vol. 2, part 2, 93.

Eight: As a Father Has Compassion

1.   Spurgeon, *The Treasury of David*, vol. 2, part 2, 275.
2.   Lewis, *Reflections on the Psalms*, 93.
3.   Joseph S. Excell, "The Psalms." *The Pulpit Commentary*, vol. 8. ed. H.D.M. Spence and Joseph S. Excell (Peabody, MA: Hendrickson, n.d.), 289.
4.   Philip Yancey, *Disappointment with God* (Grand Rapids: Zondervan, 1988), 94.
5.   Richard Baker, as quoted in Spurgeon, *The Treasury of David*, vol. 2, part 2, 284-85.
6.   Lewis, *Reflections on the Psalms*, 95.
7.   Eugene Peterson as quoted in Yancey, *Disappointment with God*, 127.
8.   Albert Barnes, as quoted in Spurgeon, *The Treasury of David*, vol. 2. part 2, 287.
9.   Carol Kent, address to Heritage Keepers. Indianapolis. 29 July 2000.
10.   Brestin and Troccoli, *Falling in Love with Jesus*, n.p.
11.   Ibid.
12.   Calvin, *Calvin's Commentaries,* vol. 6. 141.

Nine: I Hope in Your Word

1   St. Augustine as quoted in Spurgeon, *The Treasury of David*, vol. 3, part 1, 132.
2.   Matthew Henry as quoted in Spurgeon, *The Treasury of David*, vol. 3, part 1,132.
3.   Spurgeon, *The Treasury of David*, vol. 3, part 1,132.
4.   Lewis, *Reflections on the Psalms,* 60.
5.   Spurgeon, *The Treasury of David*, vol. 3, part 1, 133.
6.   Ibid., 239.
7.   Richard Sibbes as quoted in Spurgeon, *The Treasury of David*, vol. 3, part 1, 244.
8.   Spurgeon, *The Treasury of David*, vol. 3, part 1, 241.
9.   William Cowper as quoted in Spurgeon, *The Treasury of David*, vol. 3, part 1, 244.
10.   Jonathan Edwards as quoted in Spurgeon, *The Treasury of David*, vol. 3, part 1, 248.
11.   John Trapp as quoted in Spurgeon, *The Treasury of David*, vol. 3, part 1, 249.
12.   Spurgeon, *The Treasury of David*, vol. 3, part 1, 242.
13.   Simon de Muis as quoted in Spurgeon, *The Treasury of David*, vol. 3, part 1, 252.
14.   Yancey, *The Bible Jesus Read*, 115.
15.   Spurgeon, *The Treasury of David*, vol. 3, part 1, 401.
16.   Matthew Henry as quoted in Spurgeon, *The Treasury of David*, vol. 3, part 1, 408.
17.   Spurgeon, *The Treasury of David*, vol. 3, part 1, 407.

Ten: I Was Made to Praise You

1.   Chambers, *My Utmost for His Highest,* January 9.
2.   Spurgeon, *The Treasury of David*, vol. 3, part 2, 258.
3.   Brestin and Troccoli, *Falling in Love with Jesus,* n.p.
4.   Calvin, *Calvin's Commentaries,* vol. 6. 215-17.
5.   A.W. Tozer, as quoted in Eldredge, *The Journey of Desire,* (Nashville: Thomas Nelson, 2000), 57.
6.   Spurgeon, *The Treasury of David*, vol. 3, part 2, 264.
7.   Francis Taylor as quoted in Spurgeon, *The Treasury of David*, vol. 3, part 2, 282.

A Personal Note From the **Author**

Heart

Oh for a heart like David's! For the past few years, I've been praying to fall more in love with Jesus. God has been answering this cry, though sometimes in difficult ways. He has allowed pain in my life, but in that pain I have clung to Him. He has also, in His tender mercy, brought the psalms into my life, in a deeper way than ever before. How they have encouraged me, comforted me, and deepened my love for Jesus.

Soul

A verse I have clung to, and which truly represents the soul of the study is:

> I rise before the dawning of the morning
> and cry for help—I hope in Your word
> Psalm 119:147 (NKJV)

Mind

How blessed you will be if you invest in the three-volume set of Charles Spurgeon's *Treasury of David*. It is the best possible resource for the psalms. I also believe that your love relationship with Jesus will be greatly enhanced by a book by John Eldredge entitled *The Journey of Desire*. My book with recording artist Kathy Troccoli, *Falling in Love with Jesus*, has an accompanying teaching video and in-depth Bible study. If you liked *A Woman's Journey through the Psalms*, you may be interested in doing *A Woman's Journey through Ruth, Esther, 1 Peter*, or *Luke*. More information can be found on my website: DeeBrestin.com

Strength

One of the best ways to apply the psalms is to use them, as Dietrich Bonhoeffer recommends, as tools for prayer. When you pray Scripture, you know you are in God's will. Whether you are full of joy, sorrow, or fear—you will find the right psalm for prayer. There is great power in praying the Word. I also encourage you to keep listening to the wonderful Integrity CD!

My prayer for you:

Father,

How I pray for my sister. May she fall more deeply in love with You. May she, daily, hope in Your Word. When life is full of pain, when troubles overwhelm her, may she wrestle with You on Your promises and be open to You. May You bend down and listen to her cry, and give her hope, comfort, and direction.

In the powerful name of Jesus,

Amen